The Comprehensive Guide to Passing the Texas Real Estate Sales Exam

Table of Contents

The Comprehensive Guide

to

Passing the Texas Real Estate Sales Exam

Real Estate Review

Classes of Property

Most property falls under the term hereditaments. This is any property that can be inherited. Hereditaments fall under personal property or real property. Real property is land and any permanent attachments, such as buildings. Personal property is not attached to the land like real property. Storage bins would be an example of personal property. It is possible for personal property to become real property if it is permanently attached to the property by articles such as bolts, plaster, screws, etc. The intent of the tenant who adds property will be considered when determining the property's class. For example, a trade fixture that is added solely for the purpose of the tenant remains the property of the tenant. Tenants must repair any damage caused by trade fixtures.

Land Characteristics

Land includes surface rights, subsurface rights, and air rights. There are both physical and economic characteristics of land.

Physical characteristics:

- **Immobility** – Land is considered immobile because it cannot be moved. Portions of land may be moved, but it cannot be moved entirely.
- **Indestructibility** – Land's indestructibility makes it a worthwhile investment. Weather will cause changes to land, but it cannot be completely destroyed.
- **Non-homogeneity** – Each portion of land is unique, lacking homogeneity. There are identifying characteristics on each portion of land.

Economic characteristics:

- **Scarcity** – Land has limited availability, which makes it scarce, and some areas have more land available than others. Scarcity increases price, which increases the value of the property over time.

- **Modifications** – Changes to the land or modifications affect the value over time. Modifications to one property will affect the value of neighboring properties. Not all modifications will increase the value of the land.
- **Fixity** – Fixity is also called permanence because it creates investment permanence. It takes time for land to pay back the initial investment that is made.
- **Situs** – The land's location, or situs, has an effect on its value. The preferences of buyers is the most influential economic characteristic to affect price.

Encumbrances

An encumbrance is anything that harms or blocks property value such as a lien or unpaid taxes. Ownerships and property rights are difficult to determine when there is an encumbrance. Types of encumbrances are:

- **Encroachment** – Encroaching is any intrusion onto the surface or in the airspace of land, and it can be caused by poor surveying. Structures that encroach on neighboring properties are examples of encroachments.
- **Easement** – The right to use another person's land for a specific purpose is an easement. A road through one person's property to gain access to another's is an example of an easement. Common easements are easement appurtenant and easement in gross.
  - **Easement Appurtenant** – Two properties with two owners may require an appurtenant. The dominant estate benefits from the easement, and the servient estate is the land that has the burden of the easement. For example, the property with the road on it is the servient estate.
  - **Easement in Gross** – Multiple land pieces being affected at the same time require easement in gross. Utilities making use of land is an example of easement in gross.
- **Liens** – A lien is a financial claim on a property or owner that is used to secure a debt. Liens may be voluntary or involuntary, depending on whether or not the owner enters the lien willingly. Mortgages are voluntary liens because the owner enters into the agreement willingly.
  - **Mechanic's lien** – A mechanic's lien is involuntary. It may initiated by those who have provided labor or materials to improve the property, such as contractors, and not been paid. There is a statuary period for notice and foreclosure. This lien is give priority over other leans besides tax liens.
  - **Foreclosure** – The legal process of selling an owner's property to pay a debt may be put on hold by the court once the owner posts a bond to pay the amount owed.
- **Judgment** – The owner's obligation of payment as determined by the court.
  - **Writ of attachment** – The order that specifies property to be sold if an owner does not comply with the judgment.
  - **Writ of execution** – The order given to a sheriff to sell a property.
- **Tax liens** – Available at the federal, state, and local level, tax liens allow the government to collect unpaid taxes by placing a lien on property. This lien has the highest priority and is enforced by the tax sale. A tax deed is given to the purchaser.

- Property tax lien – Set at the local level, property tax liens are used to cover property taxes, local taxes, or state taxes. It is also called a special assessment tax lien.
- Federal tax lien – Liens that are placed by the IRS are federal tax liens. They are used to pay income, gift, and other taxes.
- State tax lien – Processed at the state level, these liens are used for state income tax, sales tax, etc.

Property, state tax, and mechanic liens will vary slightly by state. For example, Texas varies the statute of limitations for filing liens based on the status of the individual who files the lien as original contractor, first tier subcontractor, second tier contractor, or material supplier. Other encumbrances that properties face include: marital rights, possession rights, judgments against the owner, unpaid liens, and outstanding options to purchase.

Types of Ownership

Ownership requires the seller to provide a marketable title, which means that the property is transferable. Any claims from outside parties make the title unacceptable and prevent the transfer of ownership. It is important to carefully investigate properties for any clouds or encumbrances before attempting to transfer property:

- **Title search** – This process involves investigating the county records to ascertain if the title is marketable. It provides the chain of title.
- **Chain of title** – Conducting research on the current and past title holders is the chain of title. It shows how the title has been transferred over time and if it is marketable.
- **Grantee index** – A county reference book that traces the property buyers back to the original.
- **Grantor index** – A county reference book that traces the property sellers back to the original.

Forms of Ownership:

- **Estate in severalty** – Estate in severalty is also called sole ownership. A single property holder or entity owns the title. No other owners or businesses are connected to the property.
- **Tenancy in common** – An undivided property owned by two or more people or businesses is tenancy in common. Inheritance is a common cause of tenancy in common. In Texas, joint owners are given equal interest in the property unless stated otherwise in the deed.
- **Joint tenancy** – Similar to tenancy in common, joint tenancy involves two or more parties, but it determines the rights of survivorship. Upon the death of one tenant, the interest is given to the surviving tenants. There are four unities in joint tenancy:
  - **Unity of time** – The tenants obtain ownership at the same time; no one may be added later.
  - **Unity of title** – The interest in the title is obtained in the same way as a will.
  - **Unity of interest** – The tenants share interest equally.

- o **Unity of possession** – All tenants have the same right to occupy the land in their interest.
- **Tenancy by the entirety** – In states without community property, tenancy by the entirety shares equal interest between married couples. The interest reverts to the spouse at the time of death. It requires an additional unity:
  - o **Unity of a person** – The legal view that married couples represent single units and cannot transfer ownership individually.
- **Community property** – A method of ownership recognized in Texas, community property is joint ownership by married couples who have equal interest in the property.
- **Separate property** – The property that married individuals own before marriage, as gifts, or inheritance remain the property of the individual. This is recognized in Texas along with community property.
- **Partnerships** – Typically used when property is a form of investment, partnerships allow profits and losses to be shared.
  - o **General partnership** – Also called a regular partnership, the general partnership is the most common. The partners share all debts and liability equally.
  - o **Limited partnership** – Limited partners contribute money but do not share the full liability. The general partner is still necessary and responsible for the liability and obligations.
- **Joint venture** – Two or more businesses that pool resources for a project create a joint venture. For example, a contractor, developer, and owner may create a joint venture in building a shopping center.
- **Corporations** – Entities that have rights to purchase land, transfer property, and create contracts. Corporations pay income taxes that partnerships do not have to pay.
  - o **Real Estate Investment Trust (REIT)** – Used to prevent double taxation in corporations and by passive investors, REIT purchases real property and provides interest to the investors.
- **Land trust** – Land purchased and cared for by a trustee is a land trust. The land is typically purchased to hide the identity of the owner.
  - o **Bundle of rights** – The legal rights associated with ownership is the bundle of rights. This includes interest in real land.
- **Fee simple estate** – The ownership of real property that is considered the greatest is a fee simple estate. It provides property owners with the right to rent, sell, occupy, build, demolish, limit access, mine, or extract resources.
- **Leasehold estate** – The agreement between that allows one person to occupy the real property of another for a rental fee is the leasehold estate.

Property Descriptions

Deeds require accurate descriptions of property. In order to ensure that real property is described in a manner that is recognizable, four different methods are used:

1. **Metes and bounds** – This method of description uses the boundaries and shape of the land to describe it. The surveyor moves clockwise to make the description, and permanent monuments are chosen when possible.
2. **Rectangular survey system** – Also called the public land survey system, the rectangular system was used to subdivide the land using latitude and longitude.
   - **Congressional townships** – Divisions of six square miles using the rectangular survey system.
   - **Principal meridians** – These are the 37 longitudinal lines used in the rectangular survey system.
   - **Baselines** – Latitude lines used with meridians are baselines.
   - **Township** – A township is drawn every six miles north and south of the baseline.

3. **Recorded plat** – Also called the lot and block survey system, the recorded plat is the easiest method of description. The method is useful in densely populated areas, lots, and suburbs. The subdivisions are recorded in a plat to indicate each boundary and placed in the public record.

4. **Assessor's parcel number** – The assessor's parcel number is also known as the appraisal district's account number in Texas. Each district assigns a parcel number to each parcel of land and the value is appraised. It is public record but not used as a descriptor in a deed.

Government Rights in Land

- **Escheat** – A common law that means to fall back, escheat is applied when a landowner dies with no heirs or instructions for the property. In this case, the land falls back to the ownership of the government.
- **Property taxes** – Property taxes are collected on the state, city, and county level. This is an *ad valorem* tax that is based on the value of the property. The county appraisal district determines the value and the rate determined per $100 of the value in Texas.

Federal taxation

The federal government does not charge property taxes, but the value of the property will affect federal income taxes.

- **Passive income** – Rent for property is an example of passive income. It is any cash flow from an investment.
- **Capital gain** – Any income made when a property is sold is a capital gain and subject to federal income tax. The first $250,000 of capital gains on a personal residence is exempt from tax.
- **Depreciation** – The decrease of value over time of an investment property affects taxes by allowing a cost recovery deduction of investments.

Public Controls

- **Police power** – The government may restrict use of property with police power. The laws are created to protect the public, and they include rent control, zoning, and safety codes. Losses due to police power are not compensated.
- **Eminent domain** – The government has the authority to take ownership under eminent domain. The land is used for public use such as parks, utilities, and schools. The owner is compensated for eminent domain.
  - Condemnation – Used when negotiation fails, condemnation is the process of legally taking eminent domain and paying full value for the property.
  - Severance damage – The amount paid to a property owner if a portion of land is taken under condemnation.
  - Inverse condemnation – Property owners can file suit to make the government buy damaged property. This may occur even when the government does not exercise the right to eminent domain.
  - Consequential damage – The money awarded when the government causes property damage is called consequential damage. The damages are paid but the land is not purchased.
- **Environmental hazards and regulations** – Laws to protect people and the environment are enacted on the federal and state level. Federal laws include:
  - The Clean Air Act – The act was passed in 1973 and amended in 1990. The act gives the EPA authority to monitor emissions.
  - The Clean Water Act – This act passed in 1972 authorizes the EPA to monitor water quality and issue NPDS permits to organizations that cause pollution.
  - National Environmental Policy Act (NEPA) – Signed in 1970, NEPA is monitored by the Council of Environmental Quality.
  - The Safe Drinking Water Act – Passed in 1974, the act sets standards for drinking water safety. Amended in 1986 and 1996, water sources such as lakes and rivers are also protected.
  - The Toxic Substances Control Act – Enacted in 1976, the act allows the EPA to regulate the safety of new and existing chemicals in the marketplace.
  - Residential Lead-Based Paint Hazard Reduction Act – Passed in 1992, the act is used to protect people from lead in paint, soil, and dust.

Private Controls:

- **Restrictive covenants** – Also called deed restrictions, privately limits the use of property and are often established by developers. Restrictions can include everything from structures to landscaping.
- **Homeowners association (HOA)** – Created by developers, homeowners' associations are corporations or private parties established by a real estate developer. They demand that homeowners become members, and ownership may be lost if dues are not paid.
  - Conditions – Restrictions that determine actions owners must take are conditions.

- o Covenants – Owners make promises or covenants regarding properties.
- o Restrictions – Limitations placed on the homeowner by the developer or homeowners' association

Water Rights

State law and the source of the water determine the water rights. When the water can be navigated, the ownership extends to the mean waterline at the boundary. It extends to the center of the water if it is not possible to navigate. Underground streams are governed by the same rules as surface streams if they can be discovered easily.

- **Littoral rights** – The right to use water that is not flowing such as a lake or the ocean. The rights include building, fishing, and irrigation.
- **Riparian rights** – The rights to use flowing water are riparian rights. This includes fishing and machinery. The rights are not transferable.
    - o Natural flow doctrine – The land owner has the right to use the water but not restrict the flow of it to other property.
    - o Doctrine of reasonable use – The water may be used in a way that does not prevent other property owners from using the water.
    - o Doctrine of prior appropriation – Used in Texas since 1897, the first owners of the water are given legal priority.
    - o Doctrine of beneficial use – Used in conjunction with the doctrine of appropriation, the first landowner's priority must be beneficial and the time frame reasonable.

The state issues a permit in areas where water is not abundant to ration the resource, and the use of underground water is restricted when there is limited surface water.

- **Percolating water** – The water that seeps from the surface below ground like rain water is percolating. The landowner and not the mineral owner has the rights to capture percolating water in Texas.
- **Doctrine of correlative rights** – The amount of water that one owner of a shared water source may use is limited by correlative rights.

Value and Analysis:

Value

The value of land is constantly changing. It is affected by the actions of both the buyers and the sellers. The estimated value based on the appraisal is the market value. This is the value that a buyer and seller are likely to agree on for the exchange. The market value requires an understanding of the property's condition by each party, access to normal financing in the area, and a requirement for neither party to act under duress.

- **Cost** – The cost is the money an owner pays into purchasing and altering the property.
- **Sales price** – The price that someone pays to purchase property many be less than the cost.

There are different ways to assess and assign value to property:

- **Assessed value** – The value given by the county assessor for the purpose of estimating property tax is assessed value.
- **Book value** – The depreciation of property value for tax purposes is the book value.
- **Insurance value** – The insurance assigns a maximum value that the company is willing to pay.
- **Investment value** – The amount of money that investors are willing to provide for investment properties represent investment value.
- **Loan value** – The amount of a loan that can be secured for a property is the loan value.
- **Salvage value** – This value is determined by choosing the value of structures and improvements after they are removed. This value is the cost – accumulated depreciation.

What Affects Value:

- **Environmental factors** – Any environmental changes will alter value. For example, pollution or natural disasters will cause the value to plummet.
- **Externality** – Outside factors such as interest rates, commercial construction, and education levels of residents affect value. Externalities may be positive or negative.
- **Supply and demand** – High demand and low supply increases the property value.
- **Life cycle** – Every property and neighborhood has a natural life cycle. The life cycle has four possible stages:
    - Development – The first stage is typically a time of growth.
    - Equilibrium – The value of the property reaches its height.
    - Decline – The property loses value.
    - Revitalization – The values improve with renovations.

Principles of Value

The principles of value are used in the process of appraising property values.

- Anticipation: The anticipation that the current value of a property is going to increase due to future benefits is used in appraisal.
- Assemblage (also called plottage): Blending plots of land together to create larger properties increases value.
- Change: Value is always affected by change. Physical changes are caused over time by environmental factors. Political change will affect regulations and restrictions. Economic changes are related to prosperity levels, and social changes occur with shifting demographics.

- Conformity: Similarities and conformity to neighboring properties increase the value in appraisals. This applies in personal and commercial properties.
- Competition: This principle is related to an increase in demand and profits, which increases competition.
- Highest and best use: The most profitable use that a property is legally allowed is the highest and best use.
- Law of decreasing returns: The point at which improvements no longer sufficiently increase the value of the property.
- Law of increasing returns: This occurs when improvements make sufficient contributions to the value of the property.
- Progression: The value of a property increases when it is located near highly valued properties.
- Regression: The value of a property decreases when it is located in a neighborhood of lower valued properties.
- Substitution: The maximum value of a property is determined by the value of an equal property. When an income producing property is valued, the term applied is opportunity cost, which means that the property value is equal to other, similar investments.
- Theory of distribution: This is the understanding that the property value is greater when the land, labor, capital, and management of a property are balanced.

Methods of Estimating Value or Appraisal

There are three basic methods that appraisers use to determine the value of a property. The property itself will determine which approach should be used. The three methods are market data, cost, and income approach.

Market Data

The market data approach is also called the direct sales comparison. It determines value by comparing the property to similar properties that have sold recently. The appraiser must choose three comparable properties or comps that sold in the past six months to estimate value of the appraised or subject property. The comps should have as many corresponding features as possible such as the same number of bedrooms. Adjustments may be made if there are no matching comps in the area.

Cost Approach

The cost approach is used when there are no market comps and the property will not generate income. It estimates value by deducting the accrued depreciation from the estimated cost of improvements, known as the replacement cost. Reproduction cost, which is the cost to duplicate an asset or structure, may be used in place of the replacement cost.

The depreciation that appraisers must consider includes physical deterioration, functional obsolescence, and environmental/economic depreciation. Physical deterioration is normal wear and tear, but it also includes the effect of the elements and breakdown. Functional obsolescence occurs when there is a defect in design or the design and amenities are outdated. Both functional obsolescence and physical deterioration may be curable or incurable.

- Curable – This type of depreciation may be altered with repairs.
- Incurable – This type of depreciation may not be altered by repairs.

The land value is also a crucial part in determining the overall property value.

Environmental/economic depreciation is caused by outside factors such as the environment or social factors. This type of depreciation is not curable.

Formula

Value = Replacement or Reproduction Cost – Accrued Depreciation + Land Value

Income Approach

This approach is commonly used with income properties. The income generated by the property is placed in the value as capitalization. This requires the net operating income and capitalization rate. The operating income is money left after the expenses are paid. The location of the property and the market will determine the capitalization rate.

Formula

Value = Net operating income ÷ Capitalization rate

The Purpose of Appraisal and How It Is Used

The appraisal is necessary to determine value. The value, however, is estimated by a professional who documents the findings. The appraisal affects the market value or fair market value. There are five necessary factors that determine if there is fair market value for a property:

1) The property should be purchased with cash or the equivalent. 2) The property is not on the market for an unusual time period. 3) Both the seller and buyer understand the conditions and uses of the property. 4) The seller has the right to transfer the title. 5) Neither the buyer nor seller enter the sale under duress.

Appraiser's Role

The appraiser must complete seven steps in the process of appraisal.

- State the problem – Establish the nature and purpose of the appraisal.

- Determine the kinds and sources of data necessary – Consider the property characteristics, economic and other factors, appropriate approaches, and data needed.
- Determine the highest and best use of the site.
- Estimate the value of the site.
- Estimate the property's value by each of the appropriate approaches (market data, cost, and/or income.)
- Reconcile the different values – Termed reconciliation or correlation, estimate market value using the different approaches.
- Report the value to the client in writing – Use the narrative appraisal approach (discusses the factors used and reasons for a conclusion); a form report (computer generated forms, typically used for single residences such as the Uniform Residential Report); reports written in the Uniform Standards of Professional Appraisal Practice; the self-contained report (a complete narrative appraisal); a summary report (a narrative appraisal with less detail); and a restricted report (a report with minimal information).

Competitive or Comparative Market Analysis (CMA)

In Texas, licensed real estate brokers may prepare appraisals if they follow the uniform standards and also inform potential buyers that the CMA is not an official appraisal.

Using recent sales activity to determine the CMA, the buyer and seller will have an understanding of the range of value of a neighborhood. This range provides the homeowner (seller) a more accurate picture of a realistic home asking price. Too high a price will not attract a buyer. The CMA provides a buyer with an idea of what a fair offer would be. Sellers will not negotiate when the initial offer is too low.

Financing

Mortgage, Deeds, Trusts

- **Mortgage** – The property is collateral in a mortgage. The mortgage is the promise to pay the debt borrowed to purchase the property in payments over time. The bank may take the property if the payments are not made.
  - Hypothecation – The practice where the lender retains the title as long as money is owed.
  - Defeasance clause – The clause that stipulates the deed is returned to the property owner once the mortgage is completely paid on time.

- **Foreclosure** – The judicial proceeding that separates the buyer's interest from the property if the mortgage is not paid.
- **Deed of trust** – Also called the trust of deed, this is an alternative to foreclosure used in Texas. The deed provides for non-judicial foreclosure using a third party who has the power of sale.

- **Promissory note** – The document signed by the buyer promising to pay the mortgage by a certain date and with a specified interest.

There are four different methods by which real estate is used as collateral:

- **Standard mortgage** – Also called a regular mortgage, the standard mortgage is the most common. The lender retains the deed, which is returned to the buyer when the mortgage is voided with payment.
- **Equitable mortgage** – Recognized by common law, the mortgage occurs when the property is collateral against a debt. For example, a property owner who refuses to sell and return a buyer's deposit would, legally, incur a mortgage for the amount of the debt.
- **Deed as security** – The lender is provided with interest in the property when the deed is used as collateral. The deed is returned to the borrower when the mortgage is paid.
- **Deed of trust** – Property is used to secure a loan where a third party, who is neutral, acts as trustee.
  - Release of liability – The document delivered to the borrower in a deed of trust once the mortgage is paid off in time.

Qualifying for Financing

Borrowers must qualify for financing before they are able to obtain mortgages. Income from properties are considered in commercial loans, but personal income is considered for residential loans. The income is determined by calculating the back ratio:

Back ratio = fixed monthly debt (housing and expenses)/monthly income

The front ratio is then used to determine the quality of income that a borrower has. The front ratio or front end ratio is the ratio of housing to income. The housing cost includes the PITI (principal, interest, tax, and insurance).

Front ratio = monthly housing cost/monthly gross income

Borrowers with a front ratio over 28% are not likely to be approved for a loan. When lenders calculate other fixed obligations, such as car and student loan payments, a ratio over 36% is not likely to be approved.

The type of property being purchased also affects loans. For example, there is little incentive to pay back a loan on unimproved land that is not occupied. This makes obtaining loans for this type of land difficult to obtain. Additionally, for income properties must net enough money each month to pay the amount of the monthly payments or debt service. This is determined using the debt coverage ratio.

- **Debt coverage ratio** – Also called the Debt Service Coverage Ratio (DSCR), the ratio is the net operating income divided by the annual debt service. A ratio below one is not likely to be approved for a loan.

Types of Loans

There are different types of loans available for borrowers. The loans will vary based on the market, income, circumstances, and the buyers' needs,

- **Amortized loans** – The most popular loans are amortized. With these loans, the principal and interest are paid in equal installments every month.
    - Fixed rate – The borrower may choose a fixed interest rate, which stays the same. This is popular when interest is not high.
- **Fixed loan** – Fixed loans have fixed interest rates. They typically are made to last between 15 and 30 years.
- **Balloon loan** – Balloon loans are popular with buyers who believe they will sell properties before the full payments are due. At first, payments are below normal fixed-rate loans. Over time, however, the payments "balloon" and the buyer must pay off the mortgage. The loans are typically due in 5, 7, or 10 years.
- **Adjustable rate loan** – Providing a floating interest rate, adjustable rate loans are popular when interest is high. The rate is given initially below market value, but it increases after a predetermined time period.
    - **Cap** – The maximum that an interest rate can be raised in an adjustable rate loan is a cap.
    - **Interest only loan** – Also called a term loan or straight loan, an interest only loan requires only the interest be paid off at first. The principal, however, must be paid before the mortgage ends.

Funding Sources

While there are numerous funding sources, there are only two loan types: those funded by the private sector and those guaranteed by government agencies.

Conventional Loans: Private loans that have no insurance or guarantee from the government are conventional. Conventional loans require: 1) loan applications 2) verification of funds, employment, and income 4) appraisal forms 5) closing forms.

Financial institutions that provides the loan will vary, but many mortgages are sold through the secondary market.

Loans are sold directly to borrowers in the primary market. In the secondary market, the loans are sold to investors.

Common Home Loan Purchasers in Secondary Market:

- The Federal National Mortgage Association (Fannie Mae) – The GSE provides home loans.
- The Federal Home Loan Mortgage Corporation (Freddie Mac) – The GSE guarantees mortgages for homeowners and rental properties.

Conforming Loans – Fannie Mae and Freddie Mac offer conforming loans. The loans are limited, and in 2006, the national maximum limit was $417,000. Mortgages that go over this amount are jumbo or nonconforming.

The Government National Mortgage Association (Ginnie Mae) does not buy loans like Fannie Mae. It does, however, guarantee certificates for pools, which are used for FHA, VA, and FMHA loans.

Government Programs

The FHA and VA are government programs used to help homeowners who do not have large down payments. The programs limit the risks to lenders and encourages homeownership.

VA-Guaranteed Loans: The Department of Veteran Affairs guarantees that the lender will be compensated in the case of a default. The program is only available to veterans. The VA offers 25% of the maximum Fannie Mae amount. The borrower may be able to get a loan for the full purchase price if the he or she qualifies. VA loans require funding fees that range from 1.25% to 3.30%. The size of the down payment determines the size of the funding fee. Larger down payments equal smaller funding fees.

Federal Housing Administration (FHA) Loans: These loans are administered through HUD. They offer the lender protection in the event of a default. They require FHA mortgage insurance:

- FHA mortgage insurance – The insurance premium is added to the amount of the loan. The premium is a percentage of the loan, which was 1.5% in 2005. There is also a 5% annual premium that must be paid until the mortgage is paid off completely.

Mortgage Terms

- Mortgage – Any promise made by a mortgager where land is used as collateral, in Texas it is often a deed of trust.
- Mortgager – The borrower is the mortgager.
- Mortgagee – The lender is the mortgagee.
- Foreclosure – Selling a property at auction after the mortgager defaults is foreclosure.
- Promissory note – The note signed by the borrower promising repayment is a promissory note.
- Release of lien – Issued by the lender, the release is provided when the payments are complete and removes the lien off the title.
- Late charge – Late charges are incurred by making late payments.
- Acceleration clause – Lenders may use the acceleration clause when buyers are in default. If the debt is not paid, foreclosure may begin.
- Power of sale clause – The clause in a deed of trust that allows foreclosure without judicial process is the power of sale clause. Texas does not have statutory redemption after foreclosure begins.
- Strict foreclosure – This type of foreclosure allows the property to be immediately sold.

- Deficiency judgment – Lenders may request deficiency judgment if the foreclosure does not cover the full debt.

Laws that Govern Financing

- **Regulation Z** – Also called the Federal Consumer Protection Act and the Truth in Lending Act, Regulation Z demands that lenders disclose the dollar and percentage amount to be paid. There are five trigger terms in advertising that require disclosures: down payment amount, payment number, payment periods, finance charge, additional payment amounts, and statements that there is no financing.
  - The disclosures required by trigger terms include: cash or price of loan annual percentage rate; amount of down payment; payment frequency, amount, and number; total payments or deferred price.
- **Equal Credit Opportunity Act:** Enacted in 1975, the law prevents lenders from discriminating against applicants during credit transactions on the basis of race, color, religion, national origin, sex, marital status, or age. The law also prevents discrimination when obtaining public assistance.
- **Fair Credit Reporting Act:** Created in 1970, the law protects consumers from inaccurate credit reporting. The Federal Trade Commission requires lenders to reveal the name of the reporting agency used when they refuse loans to borrowers. Negative items remain on credit reports for seven years, but bankruptcy remains on credit reports for 10 years.

Agency Laws

The Law of Agency regulates all agency relationships, which includes legal, fiduciary relationships in which one party works on the behalf of another party. Realtors need to be aware of two agency relationships:

- General Agencies – Real estate agencies may operate as general agencies when licensed agents are the general agents of brokers.
- Special Agencies – These agencies are used for special accounts so a principal can acquire advice or services from agents and brokers.

Brokers enter into agency relationships with buyers and sellers, or principals, when they allow the brokers to act on their behalf.

- **Listing agreement** – Also called the buyer representation agreement, this document establishes an agency relationship with a broker. Principals will choose one of four listing agreements.
  - **Exclusive right to sell** – This listing provides the broker with exclusive rights, and the broker will receive the commission on the sale of the property regardless of how it is sold. The price and terms are agreed upon by the buyer and broker. The broker will earn the commission if the requirements are met and the seller does not choose to sell.

- o **Exclusive agency listing** – In this listing, the seller makes an agreement with a broker similar to the exclusive right to sell. If the homeowner sells the house without the broker, however, the commission is not paid.
- o **Open listing** – Rarely used in residential properties, open listings may be made with multiple agencies. The commission is paid to the broker that sells the property at the requested price.
- o **Net listing** – Subject to misrepresentation and fraud, this listing is rarely used. The agreement allows the broker to keep all money offered over the predetermined selling price. The broker, however, must follow the law and present all offers to the seller. If a seller takes an offer below the price agreed, the broker loses the commission.

Procedures for Listing Real Estate

Agency relationship disclosures – Disclosure must occur before an agency relationship is established. The broker does not have to put the disclosure in writing, but it is helpful. The broker must reveal legally relevant information that would cause a conflict of interest such as being the seller's subagent.

Property evaluation – Agents must provide accurate and honest information about properties. Conducting CMAs will help both buyers and sellers choose the best prices. Agents also need to point out problems and advise sellers on ways to improve the property so that it will show and sell well.

Disclosure of property conditions – Latent structural defects and property defects that are known must be disclosed. A statement by the owner detailing the known condition of the property is legally required in Texas. A visual inspection is not a legal requirement, but it will help identify problems ahead of time.

Fraud and misrepresentation – Realtors commit fraud when they knowingly withhold information or lie to the client. Misrepresentation, called innocent misinterpretation, however, occurs when conveyed misinformation is not intentional.

- Misrepresentation by omission – This occurs when the realtor does not disclose defects in the property.
- Misrepresentation by commission – This occurs when the realtor provides inaccurate information.

Apparent authority – Agency relationships include apparent or ostensible authority. This occurs when a third party recognizes an agent as acting on behalf of the principal when the agent does not. This validates the actions of the agent.

Ratification – With ratification, agency is created when an offer is accepted or adopted without prior authorization.

Agency by estoppel – Agents create this type of agency by taking on authority not expressly given them. The estoppel is established if the third party believes the agent's use of authority.

Implied authority – Customs and industry practices create implied authority. Implied authority for sharing licensing and "for sale" signs is not allowed in Texas.

Agent Responsibilities to Principals

Agents need to be responsible in maintaining fiduciary responsibility and not overstep their authority. Failure to do so may lead to civil suits and disciplinary action.

Special agent – A special agent relationship is used for a specific purpose. The agent is not authorized to sign for the principal.

Fiduciary relationship – The fiduciary relationship requires the agent to act in the best interest of the principal. There are six duties that must be executed in fiduciary relationships:

- Obedience – Called faithful performance, instructions from the principal must be obeyed by the agent, and the agent must make efforts to meet all objectives.
- Loyalty – This requires the agents to place the needs of the principal over their own needs.
- Disclosure – All information needs to be disclosed to the principal. This requires investigating all information that is pertinent.
- Confidentiality – All of the information on the principal's financials, motives, and other private information must be kept confidential.
- Accounting – The funds for the principal must not be comingled into the agent's account. Comingling can result in suspension or loss of license.
- Reasonable care – Agents must be competent in the execution of their duties. Fraud and misrepresentation are not reasonable care.

Termination of Agency

Agency relationships typically end once the objective is reach. There are, however, other causes of agency termination:

- Mutual agreement called rescission
- Property is condemned
- Principal or broker become incapacitated
- Death of the principal or broker, but not a subagent
- The property is destroyed
- The owner declares bankruptcy
- The agreed upon time ends

Commission and Fees

- Sellers and buyers pay brokers in commissions and fees. The fees in the market are not fixed, which is prohibited under federal law. The principal must know that fees are negotiable.

- **Contingent/success fees** – These fees are paid after closing. They may be flat fees or percentages of the sale price.
- **Non-contingent fees** – These are hourly fees charged regardless of the outcome. Retainers fall under this type of fee.

Disclosures that are Mandated

Disclosure Forms: Property Condition

Sellers and agents must provide property disclosure forms by before closing. The contract may be voided if the disclosure form is not provided. Requirements for previously occupied, single family units are covered in Section 5.008 of the property code.

Inspection and Verifying Information

Agents should always recommend buyers get professional inspections to identify latent defects. Defects discovered by the purchaser could lead to a lawsuit.

Material Facts

Disclose all material facts that may affect the buyer's decision to purchase the property or the selling price. For example, a death on the property would be considered a material fact.

Contracts

Contracts are legal agreements that describe forbearance or performance. Performance is an action, and forbearance is refraining from action.

Contract requirements in real estate:

- Parties must be legally competent.
- The Statute of Frauds requires the contract, unless a lease is shorter than a year.
- All parties must sign the contract.
- The objective must be legal.
- The consideration must be included.
- The offer, acceptance, and notification of acceptance must be included.
- The contract must include a legal property description.

Listing Agreements

The agreement between the seller and broker to sell, lease, or trade a property is the listing agreement. The agreement must have:

- The identities of the parties involved
- Property description
- The object of the agreement

- The term, which must include a termination date in Texas
- Defined role and obligations of the agent
- Statement of compensation for the agent
- Safety clause – Protects the agent if a buyer introduced by the agent makes a purchase after the termination date.
- Marketing forums such as internet listing and multiple listing system authorization
- Subagent authorization
- Key or lockbox authorization
- Detail of how funds are received and handled
- Agreement of arbitration or mediation
- Fair housing laws compliance
- Statement of required legal provisions
- Signatures of parties involved

Legal Requirements

The listing agreement must be signed by the seller and agent. The representative under power of attorney may sign the listing.

Fiduciary Duties

The broker is responsible to execute all of the fiduciary duties once the listing is signed.

Conditions for Terminating Listings:

- The terms of the contract have been fulfilled
- Both parties choose to rescind
- The time agreed upon has past
- Broker's or seller's death
- Fiduciary duty is breached
- Abandonment

Buyer Broker Agreements

When buyers appoint exclusive buyer agents to represent them in transactions, specific information needs to be included in the listing:

- Names of both the client and agent
- The market area defined
- Explanation of how the agent is compensated
- The agent's authority
- The term
- The duties of the agent and the client
- Dispute resolution agreements

- Fair Housing, antitrust, and other notices
- Party signatures

Purchase/Offer Agreements

Defective sales contracts, also called earnest money contracts will allow either party to terminate the transaction, so understanding contract law is essential.

- **Express contract** – This type of contract expresses intent, and it may be oral or written. A real estate contract must be in writing unless it is a lease under a year.
- **Implied contract** – Contracts may be implied by the actions of the parties. They are rare in real estate.
- **Bilateral contract** – This type of contract requires an exchange of promises between two parties.
- **Unilateral contract** – A promise is made by a single party under conditions. Bonuses and real estate options are unilateral contracts.
- **Valid contract** – A contract that parties agree on and meets all legal standards is valid.
- **Void contract** – Contracts that are not legally binding are void. Neither party may enforce the contract.
- **Voidable contract** – A contract that appears legal but does not meet all legal requirements is voidable. Contracts are voidable if they involve minors or fraud is committed. In Texas, failure to disclose creates a voidable contract.
- **Unenforceable contract** – Changes in laws or a statute of limitations make contract unenforceable, even if it is valid in every other way.

Offers and Counteroffers

Contracts begin with offers from buyers. Offers must include the following information:

- The legal description of real estate and property
- Identities of all parties
- Sales price (outlines down payment and the amount to be paid at closing)
- The financing contingency along with the deadline
- Explain the contingency for the sale of the property
- Names the agent and states the fee of escrow
- Inspections made (names inspector, deadlines, and notifications)
- Lists all disclosures
- Arbitration or mediation
- Specify remedies in the case of a breach
- Compliance with FIRPTA
- Compliance with Fair Housing laws
- Compliance with other applicable laws

- Final walkthrough
- Define who takes the risk in the event of destruction
- Commission explanation
- Signatures

Offers will expire in a predetermined or reasonable time. Buyers may remove offers before acceptance.

Counteroffers are changes to the original offer, which removes the first offer.

How to Communicate Offers

All offers, counteroffers, and revocations must be in writing. Additionally, acceptance needs to be made in writing before the buyer may be notified.

If a breach or default occurs, the wronged party has specific recourses:

- Accept partial performance – The party affected may continue to honor the contract if the breach is not substantial, such as the square footage not being correct.
- Rescind the contract unilaterally – The party may choose to call off the contract.
- Sue for specific performance – The party may choose to sue to make the other party comply with the contract. For example, a buyer may sue a seller who refuses to honor a contract that has been accepted.
- Sue of monetary damage – Buyers may sue sellers if money has been spent on the property.
- Accept liquid money – The seller may sue to keep earnest money.
- Mutually rescind – Both parties agree to nullify the contract. This must be in writing.

Texas Real Estate Commission Contingencies

- Ability to obtain financing – Lender approval is required before closing on a property. The contract agreement should be established for the specific property that requires a loan.
- The Buyer's Approval for the Title – The buyer will typically enter an agreement before examining the title of the property.
- The acceptance of property conditions by the buyer – Buyers initiate inspections after negotiations, which may reveal problems before closing.

Leases

Leases are contracts between lessors and lessees. Leasing property creates a leasehold estate, which remains in effect after property is transferred to new ownership.

Options

Buyers purchase properties at a set amount in specific time frames with options. Property owners are paid in cash for the option to be considered valid. Buyers who have the right to terminate will not face a penalty if they rescind within the time allowed.

Cancellation Agreements and Rescission

Contracts typically end with objectives met, expiration, or mutual rescission. Agreements with agencies are cancelled by termination or withdrawal. If an owner terminates a right to sell listing but sells the property within the time in the agreement, the agent receives the commission.

Agents and sellers may mutually terminate agreements. If this happens, the broker may require compensation for money spent in attempts to sell the property. If the separation is not mutual, the seller and the broker should look into legal counsel to determine legal rights before taking action.

Mutual rescission is used to cancel lease and purchase agreements. Novation, which is substituting a new contract for an old one may also be used. This require referencing the original contract.

Transfer of Property

Real estate agents help buyers and sellers establish how and when a title is transferred along with the details of the deed. The title is transferred from the grantor to the grantee.

General warranty deed – This instrument is delivered to the grantee and promises that the deed is free of encumbrances.

Title Insurance

Title insurance protects buyers if errors and problems arise such as: forged deeds, deeds issued by people who are not legally competent, misfiles, heirs, discovered wills, etc.

Preliminary title reports or title commitments are made by title companies based on searching public records. Buyers with insurance are defended by the title company in the case of a legal challenge. The insurance also protects against losses connected to errors and problems.

What is necessary for title insurance?

Title insurance providers are often the third party chosen for the job of closing or escrow agent. The steps taken from the date of the contract to the closing date are:

- Checking the status of the title
- Determining the property tax status
- Checking for any judgments, liens, or other encumbrances

Deeds

The legal document that transfers property from the grantor to the grantee is a deed. Texas law dictates the following requirements in order for a deed to be valid:

- It must be written.
- The grantor must be legally competent.
- Full names and marital status must be used.

- The legal description must be included.
- A granting clause and words of conveyance must be used.
- The grantor must sign it.
- The deed must be delivered and accepted.

Types of Deeds:

- Bargain and sale deed – Also called a special or warranty deed, the grantee pays the consideration. There are no warrantees unless the grantor specifies.
- A gift deed – There is no consideration paid by the buyer in a gift deed.
- A grant deed – This is the most common deed. The deed promises that the title is good, there are no unreported encumbrances, and the title will be conveyed.
- A quitclaim deed – The interest is of the grantor is transferred, but there are no warranties.
- A sheriff's deed – This title is transferred in a public auction or after foreclosure.
- Tax deed – This is conveyed after an auction to cover taxes that are not paid.
- Deed of trust – Trust deeds are used when the property is security for a debt.

Recording Title

An acknowledged deed is signed in front of a notary before it is recorded. Legal notice of conveyance occurs when the deed is recorded, and a priority of interest is created.

Settlement Procedures

At the closing, the buyer pays the purchase amount, and possibly the:

- Insurance policy/flood insurance
- Survey
- Termite certificate

The seller must provide the following:

- Deed
- Current tax documents
- Insurance policy
- Survey maps
- Termite inspection
- Keys, etc.

Income properties require leases, operating statements, estoppel letters, and maintenance contracts.

The closing statement must be signed by the purchaser and the seller. Additionally, the deed is signed by the seller. The purchaser must also sign the deed of trust and the note.

The closing agent must keep track of the paperwork which includes copying documents and managing signatures. The closing agent must also monitor the money and send the deed and deed of trust to the courthouse.

- Table funding – Funds are released at the table in closing.

Lenders require disclosure of certain documents, termite inspections, insurance policies, and appraisals before closing.

Closing/Settlement Purpose

The closing typically occurs after the walkthrough by the buyer and the broker. The walkthrough determines that the property is in good condition. After the walkthrough, the closing broker, buyer, and seller attend the closing with the attorneys and the title company closer.

Legal Requirement

- **Real Estate Settlement Consumer Complaint (RESPA)** – RESPA was enacted in 2011 by Congress. The law covers federally regulated first-mortgage loans for one-to-four-family homes, cooperatives, and condos. Kickbacks are illegal under RESPA, and buyers have the right to choose where they purchase title insurance. Additionally, lenders are limited to two months or one sixth of property tax when collecting for a reserve account.

Properties that are guaranteed by Fannie Mac, Freddie Mac, and Ginnie Mae fall under RESPA regulations.

Tax

There is no transfer tax in Texas.

Legal or Equitable Title

- Equitable title – A title that is held until the full price of the house is paid is equitable.
- Legal title – Called fee simple ownership, the title is fully the owner's, which grants full rights, which is evidenced by a deed or other legal document.

Special Processes

Probate – The process used to handle the estate of deceased individuals is probate.

- Testate – This occurs when someone dies with a will determining what happens to his or her property.
- Intestate – Someone who does without a will is intestate.

Foreclosure is also considered a special process

Practicing Real Estate

Fair Housing and Civil Rights

Civil Rights Act of 1866 – The law was interpreted as outlawing racially discrimination when it comes to selling, leasing, or any other activities with real or personal property.

Fair Housing Act of 1968 (Title VIII): This law makes discrimination based on sex, race, color, religion, national origin, and familial status illegal when it comes to the selling or renting property. The following actions are considered discriminatory:

- Refusing to sell, which includes negotiating or renting to someone under a protected class
- Modifying terms or conditions for individuals in protected class is an act of discrimination
- Advertising or making a statement that indicates sales to members of the protected class is restricted
- Telling a member of the protected class that the property is no longer available when it is
- Informing people that members of the protected class are coming to an area to cause homeowners to rent or sell their properties
- Changing financing conditions to make the loan impossible for a member of the protected class
- Denying entrance or participation into organizations that engage in the rental or sale of residences

Protected class – The protected class is determined by HUD. This includes religion, race, creed, color, gender, ancestry, familial status, or handicap. Handicaps, according to the Fair Housing Amendment, must meet at least one of the following:

- Limiting physical or mental disability
- Record of disability
- Known to have disability

Drug use is not considered a handicap, but being in recovery falls under the domain of handicapped.

Protected family status – Any household with a member below the age of 18 falls has this protection. This includes pregnant women.

Common Violations:

- **Steering** – Also called channeling, steering occurs when buyers are steered to certain neighborhoods over others based on protected status. This includes slanting descriptions, lying about availability, downgrading neighborhoods.
- **Blockbusting** – Also called panic peddling, blockbusting occurs when panic is induced as demographics change to make buying property easier and cheaper. The properties are then marked up and sold to members of a protected class at a marked up price.
- **Less favorable treatment** – The treatment of the protected class is less favorable when they are not offered the same services or information.

Properties covered by the Fair Housing Act:

Single family home:

- It is privately owned, and the owner uses a broker or other professional.
- Private individuals do not own the property.
- The owner does not have more than three houses, or does not sell more than one property in a two-year period.

Multifamily home:

- There are five units or more
- The owner has four units but does not live in one

The Fair Housing Act does not cover:

- HUD senior housing
- Religious organization properties that are not commercial
- Owner occupied units with four or fewer units
- Restrictions of private clubs for commercial use

Where to file discrimination complaints:

- US Attorney General
- HUD (must be written)
- US District, state, or local court (for civil action)

The plaintiff must provide proof of violations.

Penalties for Violations:

- Court costs
- Punitive damages are not limited
- Injunction on property
- Fines for damages
- State penalties
- Criminal penalties

Antitrust Compliance

Business activities that place restrictions on the marketplace and limit free competition are prohibited by the Sherman Antitrust Act. Restrictions include:

- Price fixing is not allowed
- Real estate companies cannot limit their services to specific geographical areas
- Real estate companies are not allowed to boycott businesses or other real estate companies
- Organizations may not exclude qualified brokers from membership or having access to marketing and sales information.

Advertising

False information and misinterpretations are not allowed in advertising. According to law the agent or broker's name must appear in advertising. The APR must be complete according to the truth in lending law, which is required with any trigger term. Financial advertising and presentation of property are governed by the Texas Depreciative Trade Practices Act (DTPA).

Ethics

Behavior in every relationship must be both fair and ethical. The Texas Depreciative Trade Practices Act, Law of Agency segments, and Texas Real Estate Commission (TREC) Canons of Professional Development govern fiduciary duties.

Broker-Salesperson Agreements

Brokers typically employ salespeople as independent contractors. The relationship between broker and salesperson must be established by a written contract according to federal tax code. The contract must specify the following information:

- The contractor will work on his or her own schedule
- The contractor pays individual fees
- The contractor will work at chosen locations
- The contractor is paid on completion of work
- The contractor is responsible for paying federal and FICA taxes.

In addition, the contract should include the compensation agreement, and the broker must make sure the contractor's licenses are up to date.

Specialty Areas

Tenancies and Leasehold Estates

Possessory interest is passed with a lease, which allows the tenant to occupy the property. The lease requires a signature from the tenant and landlord, and it is enforceable without being recorded, but a memorandum of lease may be recorded. It is important to include a property description in the lease.

Types of leases:

- **Gross lease** – This type of lease is typically used for residential properties and apartments. The landlord is responsible for the taxes, maintenance, and insurance.
- **Net lease** – The tenant is responsible for certain expenses such as: maintenance, property tax, and insurance.
- **Office building lease** – The lease is a blend of a gross and net lease. The landlord pays the first portion of the expenses and the tenant pays the second.

- **Percentage lease** – A percentage of gross sales is paid on top of a base rent by the tenant in this type of lease.

Tenancy Types:

- **Estate for years** – The lease has an exact term and a specific date of termination.
- **Periodic estate** – The term is specific but renews automatically. An example is a month-to-month lease.
- **Tenancy at will** – The tenancy may be terminated by the tenant or landlord with notice of one rent period.
- **Tenancy at sufferance** – Similar to a tenancy at will, tenant remains at the property after the termination date with the landlord's consent. A lease may be created for a third party who assumes the role of tenant.
- **Sublease** – Tenants create subleases with third parties to possess the demised premise, but the tenant's responsibility to the landlord remains in effect. In Texas, the landlord must approve any subleases.

Property Manager and Owner Relationships

The property manager is responsible for maintaining the property for the owner. Responsibilities include creating leases, collecting rent, maintenance, and marketing.

Marketing needs to be both effective and cost effective to attract tenants. Property managers need to remember that the law of supply and demand will also affect rental properties. Once potential renters are attracted, a review and application process is necessary to ensure that suitable tenants are chosen.

Property Management Laws

Federal and state laws govern when and how applicants should be notified of the status of their application and credit report. State laws determine what is included in the lease. The information included is:

- Description of the property
- Names of the lessor and tenant
- Terms of the lease, including dates
- Rent amount, date, and grace period (if there is one)
- The obligations of the renter
- The obligations of the landlord
- Arbitration agreement
- Signature of lessor and tenant

The Lead Based Paint Disclosure Law covers properties constructed before 1978, and state laws determine whether deadbolts, smoke detectors, or sprinkler systems are required.

Common Interest Ownership Properties

Different property types will have multiple owners:

- **Cooperatives** – Owners of apartment units are stockholders who are part of a corporation. The corporation owns the property and is responsible for *ad valorem* taxes and the mortgage. Occupants have proprietary leases, which outline the *pro rata* payments for the mortgage and other expenses.
- **Condominiums** – State laws govern condominiums, which occur when buildings with multiple units are made into separate real estate owned as fee simple. An owner who defaults will only affect the unit rather than the entire building like the cooperative.
  - Condominium declaration – The percentage of ownership and the common elements are outlined in the declaration.
  - Limited common – The elements for specific units are limited common.
- **Time-shares** – A single unit has multiple units in a time-share. The owners specify times when they occupy the unit and share the expenses and maintenance costs. Fee simple and leasehold interest are used in time-shares.

Subdivisions

Tracts of land that are divided into smaller lots are subdivisions. There are multiple owners in subdivisions. Developers construct buildings and other improvements on the land to prepare for the land's sale. Local, state, and federal laws regulate subdivisions. Plats establish the lots and easements which show the utilities necessary for the subdivision.

HUD enforces the Federal Interstate Land Sales Full Disclosure Act, which applies when more than 20 acres of 25 lots are sold across state lines. Along with legal regulations, the developer may restrict land use and improvements.

Texas Real Estate Commission: Duties and Powers

General Powers

The Texas Real Estate License Commission (TREC) is established by the Texas Real Estate License Act (TRELA). TREC consists of nine members. The State Senate approves the Governor's appointments who serve six year terms. The appointees include two brokers, a public member, and a chair. The other officers are chosen in elections of the commissioners. Three of the commissioners must be unlicensed and part of the general public, six must be licensed with five years' experience in real estate, and all nine must be voting citizens of Texas. The device 3/6/9 makes remembering the ratio easier.

TREC hires an administrator as the executive assistant who runs the staff and operations. They are responsible for making sure that TRELA is enforced.

Real Estate Broker-Lawyer Committee

There are 13 members of the Real Estate Broker-Lawyer Committee, and its purpose is to create real estate contracts and addendum and revise them. Once drafted, they are approved by TREC. The

President of the State Bar of Texas is responsible for appointing six attorneys to the committee, and six brokers are appointed by the TREC. The governor appoints the final member, who is a member of the public. The attorneys and brokers serve staggered six year terms. Appointments made by the State Bar expire after two years. The member of the public serves a six-year term.

- **Promulgated** – The approval of a contract form or addendum.

Investigations and Subpoena Power

Investigations

Investigations of complaints are made by the TREC. Complaint may be made by anyone, but they should follow the following guidelines:

- They must be written.
- They must be signed.
- They must be within four years of the incident.

Licensees are typically notified of investigations. The investigations may be covert if they are approved by the TREC ahead of time.

Subpoena Investigations

TREC has the authority to issue subpoenas and request documents. The district court becomes involved if the required documents are withheld.

Subpoena Power Hearings

Licensees are entitled to hearings within 30 days of the TREC's decision to revoke or suspend a license. An appeal to the district court may be made after the hearing.

Initial hearings are headed by the TREC administrator who appoints a hearing examiner. The examiner is responsible for making findings and conclusions and sending them along with recommendations to the TREC. Failure to post bonds or pay penalties costs the licensee the right to judicial review, and the attorney general will be notified by the TREC.

Violation Penalties

Violating TRELA is a class A misdemeanor. Since legislation dating back to 1999, the violations will result in fines or time in jail.

Unlicensed Activity

A broker or real estate agent must be licensed. Unlicensed individuals who act as agents or brokers without a license are guilty of a misdemeanor. The fine is up to $1,000 each day, and it becomes more severe for corporations or limited liability corporations.

Authority for Disciplinary Actions

Chapters 1101.151 and 1101.202 of the Texas Occupations Code outline the TREC's disciplinary authority. The TREC investigates complaints and assigns the appropriate discipline. Real estate licenses may be revoked and suspended by the TREC, but the TREC does not have the authority to revoke other licenses.

Penalties

The penalties are set by the TREC administrator. Violations can result in a penalty of up to $1,000 and revocation or suspension of the license. The penalties are communicated by the TREC to the licensee.

Recovery Fund

Individuals who suffer monetary damages because of licensed or unlicensed agents in Texas may be reimbursed by the Recovery Fund, which is set aside for this purpose. Licensees pay $10 to the fund with their applications. A *pro rata* share is charged to licensees on December 31 if the fund falls below $1 million until it reaches $1.7 million. Money may be transferred from the fund to Texas's general revenue fund if the Recovery Fund is over $3.5 million or is more than the amount of payouts during the past four years.

The court will order the payment from the fund if a judgment is not paid within six months. The fund is used only when the licensee is not able to pay the damages. The most money that can be paid in on transaction is $50,000, and the most allocated for a single licensee is $100,000.

Licensing

Scope of Practice

Any individual who expects to be compensated for certain activities related to real estate requires licenses from the TREC. These activities include exchanging, transferring, renting, purchasing, selling, or leasing real estate for someone else. The individual must be licensed even if he or she does not get paid for the services provided.

Brokers and anyone who list, offer, negotiate, appraise, auction, or deal in options must also be licensed. People who sell unimproved property require licenses. Licenses are necessary regardless of how people are paid and apply to fees, salary, and commissioned positions.

Exemptions

TRELA does provide exemptions for licenses by TREC under Chapter 1101.005 for certain actions. The exemptions include:

- Owner acting on his or her own behalf
- Property manager who rents or leases for the owner
- Attorney-in-fact

- Licensed attorney at law from any state
- Public officials
- Approved or court-appointed trustees, receivers, administrators, guardians, or executors
- Anyone acting under a will, trust, or court order
- Employees of builders who sell structures for the builder's property
- Building managers for apartment complexes
- Anyone who sells, leases, or transfers plots in cemeteries
- Anyone who sells, leases, or transfers mineral rights or mining interests
- Any appraiser who is certified by the Texas Appraiser Licensing Certification Board
- Auctioneers who are licensed by the state to "call" the auction

Corporations and Limited Liabilities (LLC)

Under TRELA, corporations and LLCs are required to be licensed as real estate brokers if they perform the same services as brokers. Corporations must have designated brokers who is an officer with a real estate broker's license. The designated broker acts on behalf of the company. LLCs require partners with broker's licenses to act as designated partners. Complaints against LLCs or corporations are against the designated employees.

Nonresident Broker

The payment of referral fees to brokers in other states or other countries falls under the non-residential broker provision. A broker from Texas has the ability to pay the referral fee to a broker in another state as long as the broker is not being paid for activities in Texas. The outside broker may be paid for actions in Texas with a non-resident broker's license.

Inspectors and Appraisers

TRELA has mandatory requirements for inspectors licensed by the state. The inspectors must obey TREC, which is responsible for licensing and monitoring appraisers and inspectors, including testing, application, and enforcement.

- **Texas Structural Pest Control Act** – This act governs professionals who work pest control as well as plumbers, electricians, and carpenters. These professionals are licensed by the state to provide structural inspections.

- **Real Inspector Estate Recovery Fund** – The fund is used to reimburse individuals who lose money as a result of an inspection.

Licensing Process

There are different licensing requirements for real estate brokers and real estate sales people.

Real Estate Salesperson Requirements:

- Must be at least 18-years-old
- Must be a US citizen or legal status

- Must be a Texas resident upon application
- Prove completed education hours (210 clock/14 semester)
- Pass the licensing exam

Real Estate Broker Requirements:

- Must be at least 18-years-old
- Must be a US citizen or legal status
- Must be a Texas resident upon application
- Have a place of business in the state
- Prove completed education hours (60 semester/900 clock)
- Pass the licensing exam
- Prove two years' experience as a salesperson with 36 months of applying
- Show competence, integrity, honesty, and trustworthiness

Education

Salesperson

A salesperson must complete a minimum of 210 secondary education clock hours, which equals 14 semester hours. The hours must be made up of the following:

- 60 hours – Principles of Real Estate
- 30 hours – Law of Agency
- 30 hours – Law of Contract
- 30 hours – Elective Core Real Estate
- 60 hours – Core courses outlined by TRELA

Broker

A broker must complete a minimum of 900 secondary education clock hours, which equals 60 semester hours. Classroom hours must come to 270. Three of these hours must cover federal, state, and local laws about discrimination in housing, credit, and community reinvestment.

Examination

A state licensing exam must be completed within six months of a TREC application. Failure to pass the exam within six months requires the application to be sent again. New applications must reflect any changes to the law.

Rejection of Applications

Texas Occupations Code 1101 Subchapter H of TRELA establishes the requirements for applications. Failure to meet the legislature's requirements is a reason for rejecting an application.

Appeals

TREC sends written notification to denied applicants who have 10 days to appeal and request a hearing. TREC will then give the appellant 10 days' notice of the hearing. The applicant may appeal to the district court if the application is denied at the hearing. The hearing findings will be final if the appeal to the court is not made within 10 days.

Continuing Education
(SAE) Salesperson Annual Education

The first license must be renewed after a year. Renewal demands completing 60 core education hours. After the first renewal, the license will be valid for two years. The next renewal follows the guidelines for MCE renewals.

(MCE) Mandatory Continuing Education

A real estate broker and a salesperson who has completed the first 60 education hours must complete 15 mandatory continuing education hours. The hours are approved by TREC. Three hours must be legal and another three hours must be ethics circulated by the TREC, which were created by the Texas Real Estate Center at Texas A&M. The rest of the education hours need to be approved by the TREC. The classes may be computer based or any other system of delivery.

Place of Business

A broker's business must comply with all laws and restrictions on deeds. A post office box may be used along with the physical address but not by itself. Any changes in address must be altered with the TREC within 10 days of the move. If a broker has more than one address, a license must be kept at each location.

Change of Sponsorship to a Salesperson

A broker who revokes sponsorship from salespersons must provide written notice to the salesperson and the return of the license for the salesperson to TREC. If a new sponsor is found, the salesperson needs to notify TREC within 10 days of the previous termination notice. This requires submitting a form signed by the new broker. If a new sponsor is not found, the salesperson is given an inactive status.

Inactive Status

The Notice of Salesperson Sponsorship Termination Form filed with the TREC causes the salesperson to become inactive. This requires the broker to give the salesperson 30 days' notice in writing. When a salesperson is inactive:
- Renewal fees must be paid to TREC
- The MCE does not need be completed until reactivation
- The person is not allowed to perform any TREC regulated acts

Renewing active status requires the salesperson to take the necessary MCE classes, pay fees, and submit an application.

Standards of Conduct

Professional Ethics and Conduct

TRELA and TREC established ethical guidelines called the Canon of Professionals Ethics and Conduct to monitor ethical behavior for brokers. There are three main articles that apply to both brokers salespeople.

- **Article 1 Fidelity** – When brokers and salespeople act as agents or fiduciaries, they must observe certain obligations:
  - All parties involved must understand that the interest of the client is the main concern of the fiduciaries.
  - Although the agent's primary duty is to the client, all people in the transaction will be treated fairly and with respect by the agent.
  - Personal interests will not supersede the client's interests.
  - The agent will perform functions meticulously and be meticulous and be faithful and observant when working on the client's behalf.
- **Article 2 Integrity** – The agent will take care to behave with integrity and avoid all misrepresentation, both omission and commission.
- **Article 3 Competency** – The broker needs to be competent and knowledgeable. This includes:
  - Continuing education and understanding market conditions and their impact on real estate is necessary for competency.
  - Brokers need to exercise judgment and remain aware of development and other relevant issues on the national, state, and local levels.

Fiduciary Duties:

- **Faithful performance** – Also called the duty of obedience, the duty requires the agent to obey legal instructions from the principal to the best of his or her ability and work conscientiously to meet objectives.
- **Loyalty** – The agent is responsible for placing the interest of the principal above his or her own. This requires notifying the principal if there is any information that may affect the value or sale of the property. In a similar vein, brokers must inform buyers of information that affects a property even if it means losing a sale.

Disloyal actions that lead to discipline according to TRELA:

- Any conduct that would be considered bad faith, untrustworthy, or dishonest
- Leasing or offering property for sale without the owner's consent or knowledge, or accepting unauthorized terms.

- Profiting on the expenditures for the principal, or charging, accepting, or receiving a commission rebate.
- Being compensated by more than one party without all parties consenting or not making a transaction clear to all parties.

- **Reasonable care** – The agent exercises reasonable care by showing expertise and competence. All material facts and information must be disclosed to principals without misrepresentation. Anything may be a material fact, so all information should be passed on to the principals. The principals should be advised to get expert guidance when necessary, and the agent should stay informed on current issues such as law, financing, and market conditions.
- **Accounting** – Brokers must deposit the client's money into a trust account or provide it to an escrow officer. The money for the principal goes directly into this account unless it belongs in the escrow, attorney, or title company's trust account. Earnest money must be deposited to the escrow agent before closing on the second day, according to the TREC.

  The trust account may not be a personal account, and all the money in the trust account must be accounted for accurately. Comingling client and personal funds can result in a license being suspended or revoked.

Single Act

Anyone who acts as a broker without a license is guilty of violating TRELA. The law simple states that one violation is as actionable as numerous violations and may result in TRELA penalties and civil suits.
- **Treble damages** – Meaning three times, treble damages may be assigned to single act violations.

Grounds for Revocation and Suspension

A licensee who commits the following can face TREC suspension or revocation:

- Being found guilty of felony, fraud
- Uses fraud or material misrepresentation on the application
- Uses fraud or material misrepresentation in personal property dealings
- Bounces a check to TREC and does not cover the cost
- Violates or ignores TRELA

A licensee who is guilty of the following while in the office of licensee may face suspension or revocation:

- Misrepresenting or not disclosing a material defect
- Promising what cannot be delivered, in ads or by other means
- Not revealing who the license represents and who is compensated to all parties
- Comingling funds or not keeping track of participants' funds
- Paying a commission or fee to an unlicensed individual

- Not placing a termination date in a buyer representation agreement or listing
- Making undisclosed profits on expenditures or taking undisclosed commissions
- Not revealing the licensee status when the principal requests it
- Promising resale profits
- Offering or placing lease or sale signs on property without the express consent of the property owner
- Encouraging someone to break a real estate contract
- Trying to negotiate with an owner or lessor who already has a written agreement with a broker
- Using false or misleading advertising
- Presenting an invoice or statement of account that is not accurate
- Threatening to take legal action that is not justifiable
- Asking unlicensed employees to perform duties that require licensing
- Not providing copies of documents to those who sign them
- In writing, not advising a buyer to purchase title insurance or have an attorney examine the abstract
- Dishonest, negligent, bad faith, or incompetent actions
- Distributing funds from escrow or trust accounts early, or not placing money in custodial trust or title company escrow account before the end of the second business day once the contract is signed
- Not providing information or documentation requested by TREC
- Not providing instruments or documents to an owner unless there is legal cause
- Any acts of discrimination based on color, race, religion, ancestry, national origin, or sex

Unlawful Law Practice (Code 1101.654)

Unless a real estate licensee is legally permitted to practice law, he or she may not give legal advice or create documents with definitions of legal remedies or rights. It is not practicing law to complete forms created or approved by the TREC. Any changes to contracts, deeds, wills, deeds of trust, etc. are considered practicing law.

Trust Accounts

Brokers who hold client funds, such as earnest money or security deposits, maintain escrow accounts. Sales people are not authorized to maintain escrow accounts, and they must deposit funds into brokers' accounts. TREC requires account information on escrow funds to be kept for four years, and any broker found guilty of comingling escrow funds is subject to disciplinary action under by TREC.

Splitting Fees

Brokers are not allowed to share fees or commissions with unlicensed individuals. Fees may be shared with licensed brokers in other states if the brokers do not negotiate in Texas. It is permissible to give unlicensed individuals gifts of no more than $50, but they may not be given cash gifts. Principals may be given fee rebates if the client consents.

Agency Brokerage

Disclosure

Brokers may only act as agents for more than one party in a transaction if all of the relationships and potential conflict of interest have been revealed to everyone involved. According to 2005 legislation, the broker acts as a TRELA intermediary when representing both the buyer and the seller. The agent must follow the guidelines for an intermediary.

Intermediary Practices

Permission for the broker to represent both the buyer and the seller, and act as in intermediary, must be given in writing by both parties. Intermediary actions are established in TRELA Texas Occupation Code 1101.558, 1101.559. 1101.560, 1101.561:

- The written consent to act as intermediary must include how and by whom the broker is to be paid.
- The intermediary may not reveal that the owner/landlord will take a lower price or the buyer/tenant will pay a higher price.
- The intermediary may not share confidential information or information the client instructs in writing to be kept private. This information may only be share in case of a court order, TRELA disclosure, or if it relates to property condition.
- Licensed appointees may assist the broker if permission is given in writing. The appointees must keep all of the information confidential. The licensee may offer opinions to the party to whom he or she is assigned. The principals will receive written notice of appointments and appointees.
- The intermediary may not offer advice or opinions and risk losing a position of neutrality. The broker is not allowed to work with a single party when serving as intermediary.

Duties to the Client

The mnemonic device OLD CAR will help you remember fiduciary duties to the client:

- **O**bedience
- **L**oyalty
- **D**isclosure
- **C**onfidentiality
- **A**ccounting
- **R**easonable and due diligence

The Canons of Professional Conduct established by TREC are: fidelity, integrity, competency.

Broker/Salesperson Relationships

Salespeople work as independent contractors or brokers sponsor them. The brokers guide the actions of employees. In the case of private contractors, however, the broker can only assign what must be done. How, when, and where it is done is up the discretion of the contractor. The salesperson/broker relationship should be outlined by a written working agreement that also includes how the salesperson should be compensated.

The Broker's Responsibility for the Actions of Salespeople

Brokers are responsible for their own actions as well as the actions of their salespeople. They are not responsible for the actions of subcontractors or other licensees. Brokers are also responsible for reporting any falsified information, concealment, or misinterpretation of facts by licensed individuals. The broker is liable if he or she does not report misconduct of licensees.

Contracts
Standard Contract Forms

When promulgated forms or forms approved by the TREC are not used, they must be prepared by attorneys or principals. Licensees may not provide advice on the forms created by principals. Opinions or advice about the title may not be expressed.

Statute of Frauds

The statute establishes that contracts are only enforceable if they are in writing. Verbal agreements are not binding. Enforceable documents include: Offers, acceptances, land contracts, binders, escrows, deeds, and options to purchase.

Special Topics

Community Property

According to Texas law, married couples share ownership of real land and property equally. All property acquired during a marriage is community property. The property rights end when the marriage legally dissolves. It is possible for couples to create separate property in writing before or during marriage. The attempt to partition property requires legal counsel. If a separate property is income generating, the money could become community property, unless both parties agree that it remains separate.
- **Separate property** – This is not community property, and it includes any property acquired before or after marriage.

Homestead

In Texas, any home occupied by two or more people becomes a homestead. Borrowed from Spanish law, the homestead is used to protect the property owner. The homestead is exempt from ordinary debt and most creditors.

Liens that may be placed on homesteads are:
- Tax liens
- Mortgages
- Mechanic's and materialman's liens, when made correctly
- Homeowners association liens
- Homeowner equity liens, when made correctly

Rural homestead – The homestead has a maximum of 100 acres for a single person and 200 acres for a family of two or more. The property does not qualify as a rural homestead if it is incorporated when purchased.

Urban homestead – The land must be 10 acres or fewer and used as the primary residence. This may be incorporated or unincorporated and includes improvements.

Exempt personal property – Exempt personal property may accompany exempt real property. The maximum value for a single homestead is $15,000 and $30,000 for a family homestead.

Deceptive Trade Practices Act

Passed in 1973, the Deceptive Trade Practices Act (DTPA) is a consumer protection law. The law protects any purchasers of goods, such as real or personal property, or services. The law prohibits breaches of warranty, unconscionable actions and misleading or deceptive actions. There is a "laundry list" of 25 violations, many of which are mirrored in TRELA. Consumers may recover up to three times their loss from a court order under DTPA. Only TREC make revoke a license.

Descent and Distribution

After a person dies intestate, without a legal will, the state laws govern distribution of assets. Intestate succession also called title of descent makes the exact distribution among eligible beneficiaries.

Intestate Succession

In Texas, property that is intestate is transferred by the probate court in the owner's county. The court allocates property to heirs and beneficiaries if it is not legally obligated to pay creditors. The majority of the assets will be awarded to a spouse and children. The bulk of the estate will go to grandchildren if there are no surviving children or a spouse. In the event that the individual dies without any direct descendants, the estate reverts to parents, and siblings and their children.

- **Escheat** – The doctrine in which the estate of a person with no heirs falls to the state.

Seller Disclosure Requirements

Section 5.008 of the Texas Property Code (TPC) was added in 1993. This law demands that anyone who sells a previously occupied home provide written description of the property's condition. This notice must be provided before the signing of the contract, or the buyer has the right to terminate the agreement within the first seven days of delivery. The buyer has the right to terminate the agreement up to the closing date if the notice is not received.

Exemptions from TPC Section 5.008

- A bankruptcy trustee
- A foreclosure sale or court order
- To a mortgage by mortgagor or a successor in interest; to the beneficiary of deed of trust by a successor in interest or trustee
- A beneficiary of a deed of trust or mortgagor who bought the property as a deed of trust from a court ordered foreclosure, or bought property by deed in place of a foreclosure
- A fiduciary who is administering the estate as part of a trust, conservatorship, or guardianship
- One co-owner to other co-owners
- To a spouse or those in the lineal line of a single transferor or multiple transferors
- Between spouses in the event of a legal separation or dissolution of marriage or in the event of a property settlement as a result
- To or from government entities
- Transferring new residences or single dwelling units that have not been occupied
- Transferring any real property when the dwelling is below the property value by 5% or more

Landlord and Tenant Issues (Section 411.118)

- Employers at residential units who require employees to operate vehicles may access DWI conviction history of employees.
- The notice to vacate may be placed on the exterior of the main entry if there is not an accessible mailbox or the landlord is not able to enter because of a bolt, alarm, or animal.
- Under the writ of possession, the tenant must be notified by the court in writing, and it must be sent by first class mail. When the officer executes the writ, the warning should be posted on the front door. The warning must list the date and time of the action, which must be at least 24 hours after the posting.
- All landlords have the duty to assuage damages when a tenant violates the lease by abandoning the property.
- Tenants may deduct rent to pay for repairs if the landlord does not provide them. The deduction may equal $500 or a month's rent, whichever is higher. Rent may only be withheld if the criteria are met. Tenants will terminate their rights if they do not pay and the criteria are not met.

Foreclosures

Buyers who have mortgages in Texas are given the title, which makes strict or judicial foreclosures difficult for creditors. Many lenders choose a deed of trust, using a third party as a trustee. The foreclosure occurs under the "Power of Sale" clause. The following procedures are used for the statute:

- The borrower in default will be notified in writing and given 20 days to pay the deficiency so that the loan can be reinstated.
- If the borrower remains in default after notification, the lender will have the trustee accelerate the note, resulting in foreclosure.
- The trustee will contact the borrower and post notice at the courthouse. The notice that the property will be auctioned must be posted a minimum of 21 days before the sale.
- The auction of the property must take place on the first Tuesday of the month after the notice is posted between the hours of 10:00 am and 4:00 pm.
- The money from the sale pays the legal fees, trustee's fees, and sale costs first. The remainder is used to pay the interest and outstanding balance of the loan.
- Any money left belongs to the owner of the property.

Recording Statutes

Real estate documents must be written in English and acknowledged before they are recorded. Documents must be recorded in the courthouse in the same county as the property. The documents recorded provide protection for the public. They offer legal notice or constructive notice in real property to prevent fraud.

Mechanic's and Materialman's Liens

- Before a homeowner signs a contract for construction, the original contractor must provide the homeowner information disclosing the owner's rights.
- Before construction, the original contractor must create a list of suppliers and subcontractors and deliver it to the owner.
- When third party financing is paying for the construction, the documents from the lenders need to be given to the owners one business day before the closing date.
- A list of all the bills the contractor wishes to be reimbursed for must be provided in a statement signed by the original contractor and given to the owner.
- If a lender pays the contractor directly, the lender is responsible for providing the owner with a statement of funds that outlines what funds are being dispersed and how they are dispersed.
- The owner must be given an affidavit by the original contractor that states all subcontractors have been paid before final payment can be made.
- Failure to comply will result in a fine of $4,000, a year in jail, or both.

Property Tax Consulting

Property tax consultants have requirements established by the Texas State Board of License and Regulation. In tax disputes over single-family residences, however, real estate licensees do not need to register as tax consultants to represent the owners. When doing so, it is imperative that the licensees not represent themselves as tax consultants.

Real Estate Math

The Real Estate Math section of this guide should not be taken lightly. Most state exams include around 10% math questions, but you don't have to be a mathematician to effectively complete this part of the test. Use this review to refresh your understanding of arithmetic, algebra, geometry, and word problems. You will also have the opportunity to practice with the sample problems included for each math topic.

Some of the math question types you may come across on your exam include:

- Area
- Percentages
- Property tax
- Loan-to-Value Ratios
- Points
- Equity
- Qualifying Buyers
- Prorations
- Commissions
- Proceeds from sales
- Competitive Market Analyses
- Income Properties
- Depreciation

Use the following to help you complete the math questions.

Tips for Completing Math Questions

Before taking the exam, and specifically before completing the math portion of the exam, there are a few things you may want to keep in mind:

Leave No Question Unanswered

Although you may not know the answer to every question right off the top of your head, it is advisable that you answer every question to the best of your ability. You immediately have a 1 in 4 chance of getting the answer correct. There are also some instances where an answer choice is clearly not correct, which improves your chance for selecting the right answer.

Use a Calculator

Texas allows the use of calculators that are non-programmable, silent, battery-operated, and that do not have printing capabilities and do not have an alphabet on the keyboard. You shouldn't solely rely on the calculator as this can slow you down, but using it to work out some mathematical equations can prove to be very helpful.

Utilize Scrap Paper

Let nothing take the place of scrap paper. While using a calculator can help you get the answer quickly, writing your thought process on scrap paper provides information for you to refer to in case you get stuck.

Review! Review! Review!

Avoiding an incorrect answer can be something as simple as checking your work.

Math Review

Basic math skills in the areas of arithmetic, algebra, geometry and word problems will be necessary. Here's a review.

Arithmetic

Multiplication

"Factor" is the term used to describe the two numbers that are being multiplied. The answer is known as the product.

Example:

2 x 5 = 10   2 and 5 are the factors. 10 is the product.

A multiplication problem can be presented in a variety of ways.

1. You may see a dot between the two factors, which denotes multiplication:

   $2 \cdot 5 = 10$

2. The use of parentheses around a part of one or more factors denotes multiplication:

   (2)5 = 10
   2(5) = 10
   (2)(5) = 10

3. A number next to a variable denotes multiplication:

2a = 10

Multiply "2" and "a" to arrive at the product of 10.

Division

The divisor is the number "divided by," while the dividend is the number the divisor is going into. The result is the quotient.

Division is similar to multiplication by the fact that there are several ways to present the problem.

$12 \div 3 = 4$

$12/3 = 4$

$\dfrac{12}{3} = 4$

Decimals

The key to understanding decimals is knowing each place value.

Here is a table to help you remember:

4	6	3	2	6	.	5	7	9	1
Ten Thousands	Thousands	Hundreds	Tens	Ones	Decimal	Tenths	Hundredths	Thousandths	Ten Thousandths

Using the above table, this number would be expressed as: 46,326.5791

It is also important to understand how to round decimals. If the number immediately following the number you must round is 5 or greater, you increase the preceding number by 1. If the number immediately following the number you must round is less than 5, drop that number and leave the preceding number as is.

Example:

0.236 = 0.24

0.234 = 0.23

Adding Fractions

Adding fractions with like denominators is a simple operation. You add the numerators together and leave the denominator as it appears.

Example:

$$\frac{3}{5} + \frac{1}{5} = \frac{4}{5}$$

Adding fractions with unlike denominators requires you to find the least common denominator. The least common denominator is the smallest number that each of your denominators can divide into evenly.

Example:

$\frac{4}{6} + \frac{3}{4}$ The least common denominator is 12 because 6 x 2 = 12 and 4 x 3 = 12

Once you have determined the least common denominator, each fraction should be converted to its new form. This is done by multiplying the numerator and denominator by the appropriate number in order to arrive at the least common denominator. Next, you add the new numerators, which gives you the final answer.

Example:

$$\frac{4}{6} + \frac{3}{4} = \frac{2(4)}{2(6)} + \frac{3(3)}{3(4)} = \frac{8}{12} + \frac{9}{12} = \frac{17}{12}$$

Subtracting Fractions

Subtracting fractions with like denominators is a simple operation. You subtract the numerators and leave the denominator as it appears.

Example:

$$\frac{3}{5} - \frac{1}{5} = \frac{2}{5}$$

Subtracting fractions with unlike denominators requires you to find the least common denominator. The least common denominator is the smallest number that each of your denominators can divide into evenly.

Example:

$\frac{8}{9} - \frac{3}{6}$ The least common denominator is 18 because 9 x 2 = 18 and 6 x 3 = 18.

Once you have determined the least common denominator, each fraction should be converted to its new form. This is done by multiplying the numerator and denominator by the appropriate number in order to arrive at the least common denominator. Next, you subtract the new numerators, which gives you the final answer.

Example:

$$8/9 - 3/6 = 2(8)/2(9) - 3(3)/3(6) = 16/18 - 9/18 = 7/18$$

Multiplying Fractions

When multiplying fractions, the denominators of the fractions can be alike or different. Either way, the operation is performed the same.

Multiply the numerators and denominators.

Example:

$$4/7 \times 3/5 = 12/35$$

Dividing Fractions

When dividing fractions, you actually multiply the fractions by their reciprocals.

You find the reciprocal of a number by turning it upside down. For example, the reciprocal of $3/8$ is $8/3$.

Solve the problem.

$$18/24 \div 2/4 = 18/24 \times 4/2 = 72/48 = 3/2$$

Percent

"Percent" is used to describe a portion of a whole, with the whole being 100.

How do I change a decimal to a percentage?

This operation is simple. Move the decimal two places to the right of the number, add a percentage sign, and voila!

Example:

.32 = 32%

.04 = 4%

.1 = 10%

How do I change a fraction to a percentage?

The first step in converting a fraction to a percentage is to change the fraction to a decimal. Do so by dividing the denominator into the numerator. From here you move the decimal two places to the right of the number, and then add the percentage sign.

Example:

= .5 = 50%

= .25 = 25%

How do I change a percentage to a decimal?

Simply slide the decimal two places to the left of the number and take away the percentage symbol.

Example:

69% = .69

4% = .04

How do I change a percentage to a fraction?

Divide the number by 100. Reduce to lowest terms.

Example:

$25\% = {}^{25}/_{100} = {}^{1}/_{4}$

$62\% = {}^{62}/_{100} = {}^{31}/_{50}$

How do I change a percentage that is greater than 100 to a decimal or mixed fraction?

To change to a decimal:

Add a decimal point two places to the left of the number –

298% = 2.98

600% = 6.0

980% = 9.8

To change to a mixed fraction –

$275\% = \frac{275}{100} = \frac{200}{100} + \frac{75}{100} = 2 + \frac{3}{4} = 2\frac{3}{4}$

$275\% = 2\frac{3}{4}$

$550\% = \frac{550}{100} = \frac{500}{100} + \frac{50}{100} = 5 + \frac{1}{2} = 5\frac{1}{2}$

$550\% = 5\frac{1}{2}$

Conversions Commonly Seen in Real Estate:

Fraction	Decimal	Percentage
½	.5	50%
¼	.25	25%
1/3	.333…	33.3…%
2/3	.666…	66.6…%
1/10	.1	10%
1/8	.125	12.5%
1/6	.1666…	16.6…%
1/5	.2	20%

Algebra

Equations

To solve an equation, you must determine what is equal to the unidentified variable.

Things to remember about equations:

4. There are two parts to an equation. They are separated by an equal sign.

5. An operation performed in an equation must be done in each part.

6. When beginning to solve the equation, priority #1 is to get the variables on one side and numbers on the other.

7. You will usually have to divide both parts of the equation using the coefficient. This will enable the variable to equal an exact number.

How do I check an equation to make sure it is correct?

Once you've solved the equation, take the number equal to the variable and input into the original equation.

Example:

$x = 15$

Original equation: $\dfrac{x}{3} = \dfrac{x + 35}{10}$

$$\dfrac{15}{3} = \dfrac{15 + 35}{10}$$

$$\dfrac{15}{3} = \dfrac{50}{10}$$

$$5 = 5$$

Algebraic Fractions

Example:

How do I solve subtraction on two fractions with different denominators?

$$\dfrac{x}{6} - \dfrac{x}{12}$$

$$\dfrac{x\,(2)}{6\,(2)} - \dfrac{x}{12}$$

$$\dfrac{2x}{12} - \dfrac{x}{12} = \dfrac{x}{12}$$

Geometry

Terms to remember:

1. **Area** – Refers to the space inside a two-dimensional figure.

2. **Circumference** – Refers to the linear distance around a circle.

3. **Perimeter** – Refers to the total distance around a two-dimensional figure.

4. **Radius** – Refers to the distance from the center point of a circle to its perimeter.

Area

Area refers to the space inside a two-dimensional figure.

In the triangle below, the area is the part that is shaded green.

 ▦ = **Area**

Area Formulas for Various Shapes

Circle: $A = \pi r^2$

Sphere: $A = 4\pi r2$

Rectangle: $A = lw$

Square: $A = s^2$

Triangle: $A = \dfrac{1}{2} bh$

Parallelogram: $A = bh$

What do the above letters/symbols mean?

A: Area

π: 3.14

r: Radius

l: Length

w: Width

s: Side length

b: Base

h: Height

Examples of area:

Area of circle   **Area of rectangle**

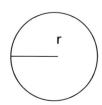   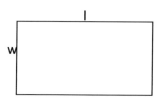

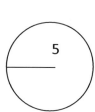

A = πr²   A= lw

A = π x (5x5)   A = 8mm x 3 mm = 24 mm²

A = π x 25

A = 3.14 x 25

A = 78.54

Perimeter

Perimeter refers to the total distance around a two-dimensional figure.

It is simply calculated by adding together all of the sides of the figure.

Example:

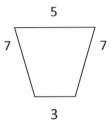

Perimeter = 7 + 7 + 5 + 3 = 22

Circumference is the perimeter of a circle.

Formula for circumference: C = 2πr

Word Problems

Understanding word problems is crucial to doing well on the math problems of the Real Estate Exam, as these make up a significant portion of the math problems found on the exam.

Before knowing how to solve the problems, you must understand what the problem is asking.

Terms you will commonly see:

1. **Increase**

   What operation do you perform?
   Answer: Addition

   Example:
   A number is increased by 7, which means x + 7.

2. **Less than**

   What operation do you perform?
   Answer: Subtraction

   Example:

A number less than 12, which means 12 − x.

3. **Product or times**

What operation do you perform?
Answer: Multiplication

Example:
A number times 8, which means x (8).

4. **Times the sum**

What operation do you perform?
Answer: Multiply a number by a quantity

Example:

Six times the sum of nine and a number, which is 6(9 + x).

5. **Of**

What operation do you perform?
Answer: Multiplication

Example:

5% of 100 is 5, which means 5% x 100 = 5.

6. **Is**

What operation do you perform?
Answer: Equals

Example:

10 is 20 minus 10, which means 10 = 20 − 10.

7. **The use of two variables**

What operation do you perform?
Answer: Whatever the equation states

Example:

A number y exceeds 3 times a number x by 8, which means y = 3x + 8.

Creating and Using Variables in Word Problems

In order to solve some word problems, you may be required to create and use variables. The first step in doing so is to determine what you know and don't know regarding the equation.

Examples:

Perry made $5 more than Billy in his paper route.
What do you know? Perry made $5 more
What don't you know? The amount that Billy made
So,
The amount Billy made is x and the amount Perry made is x + 5.

Pam made 3 times as many A's on her report card as Jan.
What do you know? Pam made 3 times as many A's as Jan
What don't you know? The number of A's that Jan made
So,
The number of A's Jan made is x and the number of As Pam made is 3x.

Greg has 4 more than 2 times the number of marbles that Shelly has.
What do you know? Greg has 4 more than 2 times the number of marbles Shelly has
What don't you know? The number of marbles Shelly has
So,
The number of marbles Shelly has is x and the number of marbles Greg has is 2x + 4.

Percentage Word Problems

There are three main types of percentage word problems. All three types follow the same formula for calculating the result.

Formula:

$$\frac{\#}{part} = \frac{\%}{\_\_\_\_}$$

whole   100

Calculate the problem substituting the appropriate information in the above formula.

Keep this in mind:

8. On the percentage side, 100 will always be the denominator.

9. If you are not provided with a percentage amount to use as the numerator, use a variable.

10. On the number side, the number always equals the whole (100%). In the word problem, this number follows the term "of."

11. On the number side, the numerator is the number that's equal to the percent.

Examples:

How do you find the percentage when you know the number?

What is the number that is equal to 40% of 95?

$$\frac{\#}{\quad} \qquad \frac{\%}{\quad}$$

$$\frac{x}{95} \ = \ \frac{40}{100}$$

Cross multiply:

100(x) = 40(95)

100x = 3800

$$\frac{100x}{100} \ = \ \frac{3800}{100}$$

x = 38

Answer: 38 is 40% of 95

How do you find the number when you know the percentage?

40% of what number is 38?

#	%

$$\frac{38}{x} = \frac{40}{100}$$

Cross multiply:

100(38) = 40(x)

3800 = 40x

$$\frac{3800}{40} = \frac{40x}{40}$$

95 = x

Answer: 40% of 95 is 38

How do you find what percentage one number is of another?

What percentage of 95 is 38?

#	%

$$\frac{38}{95} = \frac{x}{100}$$

Cross multiply:

100(38) = 95(x)

3,800 = 95x

$$\frac{3,800}{95} = \frac{95x}{95}$$

40 = x

Answer: 40% of 95 is 38

Calculating Rate

Calculating cost per unit, interest rate and tax rate are common problems found on the real estate exam. The purpose of rate is to compare two amounts, using various units of measure.

Rate formula: $\dfrac{x\ units}{y\ units}$

Calculating cost per unit

Example:

How much do 2 square feet cost if 250 square feet cost $2,500?

Answer:

$\dfrac{2,500}{250}$ = $10/square foot

Therefore, 2 square feet cost $20

Interest rate

The formula for simple interest is:

Interest = principal x rate x time

Basic Percentage

Determining basic percentage.

Example:

How do you calculate 53% of $3,645?

Answer:

Convert 53% to a decimal by moving the decimal two units to the left of the number.

53% = .53

Multiply the result by $3,645.

(.53) (3,645) = $1,931.85

$1,931.85 is 53% of $3,645.

Percentage: Interest

How do you calculate the rate of interest being charged?

Example:

Paul Billings borrowed $22,000. He is paying $1,200/year in interest. What is the interest rate he is being charged?

I = principal x rate x time

The principal amount is $22,000

The interest amount is $1,200

Rate = x

Time = 1 year

Using the formula, Interest = principal x rate x time, solve for x.

1,200 = 22,000(x)(1)

1,200 = 22,000x

$$\frac{1,200}{22,000} = \frac{x}{22,000}$$

.055 = x

Convert the decimal to a percent. Do this by moving the decimal two places to the right.

.055 = 5.5%

Area of Various Figures

Rectangles

Keep in mind: The formula for area in a rectangle is: Area = (length) (width)

Example:

Theresa purchased two small lots of land. One is 70 feet by 20 feet and the other, 80 feet by 30 feet. What is the total square feet of land that she has?

Answer:

A = (70) (20) + (80) (30) =

A = 1,400 + 2,400 = 3,800 square feet

Theresa has a total of 3,800 square feet in land.

How do you find the length of a rectangle if you only know the area and width?

Keep in mind: The formula for area in a rectangle is: Area = (length) (width)

Example:

Theresa has 2,400 square feet of land that is 30 feet in width. What is the length of the land?

Answer:

2,400 = (x) (30)

$$\frac{2,400}{30} = \frac{(x)(30)}{(30)}$$

$$x = \frac{2,400}{30}$$

x = 80 feet

Triangles

Keep in mind: The formula for area in a triangle is: Area = bh

Example:

For their small business, Paul and Sally Green are buying a triangular piece of land. The base of the property is 150 feet. The side that is perpendicular to the base is also 150 feet. What is the total number of square feet for the property?

Area = x

Base = 150

Height = 150

x = (or .5) (150) (150)

x = (or .5) (22,500)

x = 11,250 square feet

Circles

Keep in mind: The formula for area in a circle is: $A = \pi r^2$

Example:

Gill is using a circular prop on a circular piece of land for a special project. The radius of the circular land area is 23 feet. What is the area of the prop?

For "π", use 3.14.

What do you know?

Radius = 23

π = 3.14

Area = x

Solve.

$A = \pi r^2$

A = (3.14) (23)(23) = 1,661.06 square feet

The area of the prop is 1,661.06 square feet.

Loan-to-Value Ratios (LTV)

Problems regarding loan-to-value ratios typically involve percentages.

A mortgage loan for 20% is at an 85% LTV. The interest on the original balance for one year is $21,474. When securing the loan, what was the value of the property? Round to the nearest penny.

Solve.

Step #1: Determine the loan amount.

What do you know?

20% of the loan amount is $21,474.

Loan amount = x

In equation form this means:

($21,474) = (20%) (x) OR ($21,474) = (.2) (x)

$$\frac{21,474}{.2} = \frac{.2x}{.2}$$

x = $107,370

The loan amount is $107,370

Step #2: Determine the value of the property.

What do you know?

Loan amount = $107,370

Loan-to-value ratio = 85%

Value = x

$107,370 is 85% of the value

In equation form this means:

(85% or .85) (x) = $107,370

$$\frac{.85x}{.85} = \frac{107,370}{.85}$$

x = 126,317.64

The value amount is $126,317.64

Points

"Point" is the term used to describe loan discounts. Each point represents one percent of the face amount of the loan. For example, 3 points means 3% of the face amount of the loan.

Example:

Burt is attempting to obtain an $80,000 FHA mortgage loan. In order to do so, he must pay a 2-point discount (2%). What is the discount amount?

Answer:

Before solving the problem, convert the percentage to a decimal.

2% = .02

What do you know?

Amount of the loan = $80,000

Points = .02

Amount of the discount = x

x = (.02) (80,000)

x = $1,600

Equity

How do you calculate the value of a home?

Example:

John owns a home of which he has three mortgages. The first mortgage balance is $190,000. The second mortgage balance is $20,000 and the third mortgage balance, $10,000. The equity in John's home is $50,000. What is the value of John's home?

In this problem, the value of the home is the total of all three mortgages plus the equity.

Answer:

$190,000 + $20,000 + $10,000 + $50,000 = $270,000

The value of the home is $270,000.

Qualifying Buyers

Megan is attempting to qualify for an FHA loan to buy a home. Her ratio requirement is 34/41. She makes $75,000/year and has a $900 monthly car payment. What is her maximum PITI payment?

Answer:

First, divide Megan's annual income by the number of months in a year (12).

$75,000/12 = $6,250

Megan's monthly income is $6,250

Next, determine the front-end qualifier by multiplying Megan's monthly income by the front-end portion (in decimal form) of the ratio.

$6,250 (.34) = $2,125

$2,125 is the front-end qualifier

Lastly, determine the back-end qualifier by multiplying Megan's monthly income by the back-end portion (in decimal form) of the ratio. Then subtract Megan's debt amount from this number.

$6,250 (.41) = $2,562.50 - $900 = $1,662.50

$1662.50 is the back-end qualifier

The maximum PITI is $1,662.50. PITI is the lower of the two qualifiers.

Prorations

During settlement, there is typically a reconciliation that needs to take place regarding money that is owed as of the settlement date. The best way to remember who owes what is by remembering the simple fact that he who uses the service is the one who has to pay for it. When calculating these figures, unless otherwise noted, you must always use a 30-day month and 360-day calendar year.

Example:

Mr. Perkins paid his 2012 property taxes in the amount of $2,400 one year in advance. He sells his house to Mr. Dickinson in April 2012 and settles in May of that same year. With regard to the amount paid in taxes, how much do the two gentlemen owe each other?

What do you know?

	Mr. Perkins	Mr. Dickinson
How many months paid for?	12 ($2,400)	0 ($0)
How many months used/will use?	4 ($800)	8 ($1,600)
How many months should he get reimbursed for?	8 ($1,600)	0 ($0)
How many months should he get reimbursement for? ($1,600)	0 ($1,600)	8

Mr. Dickinson should be debited $1,600. Mr. Perkins should be credited $1,600.

Commissions

Commission calculation problems are common. They usually seek to determine a percentage, but they may also ask for a dollar amount.

Example:

The broker made her first home sale for $127,000. The total amount of commission is $7,700. What is the broker's commission rate?

Answer:

What do you know?

Home price: $127,000

Commission: $7,700

Commission rate: x

In equation form, this means:

$127,000x = 7,700$

Solve.

$$\frac{127{,}000x}{127{,}000} = \frac{7{,}700}{127{,}000}$$

x = 0.060

Change to a decimal and round to the nearest whole percent.

0.060 = 6%

Example:

An agent made a 6% commission on the sale of a home. The sale price was $345,867. The agent made another 6% commission on the sale of a $243,542 home. What is the total dollar amount the agent received in commission on the two homes?

Determine the commission amount on the first home sale.

$345,867 (.06) = $20,752.02

Determine the commission amount on the second home sale.

$243,542 (.06) = $14,612.52

Add together the two commission amounts.

$20,752.02 + $14,612.52 = $35,364.54

Total commission = $35,364.54

Sale Proceeds

Example:

The agent is working with the homeowner to determine the list price for the homeowner's home in order to meet the homeowner's desire to net at least $30,000. The current mortgage balance is $235,000 and the commission to take into consideration is 7%. If they list and sell the property at $300,000, will the homeowner net at least $30,000?

What do you know?

Expenses: Total - $256,000

Mortgage balance: $235,000

Commission: $21,000

Sale price: $300,000

$235,000 + $21,000 = $256,000

$300,000 - $256,000 = $44,000

The homeowner will net $44,000. Therefore, he will net at least $30,000

Property Tax

Property tax questions are solved using percents and rates.

Example:

Laurie Collins lives in Purple County. The tax rate for Purple County is $5.89 per one hundred of assessed valuation. Ms. Collins shares that she pays $2,550 in taxes. What is her property assessment? Round answer to nearest 10 cents.

What do you know?

Taxes = $2,550

Tax rate = $5.89 per hundred (%)

Assessment = x

$5.89 is 5.89%. Convert the percentage to a decimal: .0589

.0589 of the assessed value of the house is $2,550, which means:

(.0589) (x) = 2,550

Solve.

$$\frac{.0589x}{.0589} = \frac{2,550}{.0589}$$

x = $43,293.718

Rounded to the nearest 10 cents, the answer is $43,293.70.

How do you determine the tax rate if you know the amount of taxes paid and assessment amount?

Example:

Mrs. Ferguson said her taxes are $1,300 and property assessment $40,000. What is the tax rate percentage?

What do you know?

Taxes = $1,300

Assessment = $40,000

Rate (%) = x

In equation form, this means:

($40,000) (x) = 1,300

Solve.

$$\frac{40,000x}{40,000} = \frac{1,300}{40,000}$$

x = .0325

Convert to a percentage.

The rate is 3.25%

Competitive Market Analyses (CMA)

CMAs help sellers get a better understanding of the market value of their property, which could in turn help them decide on the sale price. Although very useful, it is important to note that CMAs are not appraisals.

CMA problems are solved by using measurable aspects of comparable properties to come to a specific value.

Example:

Mr. Stone has the blueprint for two homes he would like to build. Home A is 62' x 94' in size and will cost $234,985 to build. Home B is 90' x 112' in size. If each house costs the same per square foot to build, how much will it cost to build Home B?

Answer:

Remember, the formula to find Area for a rectangle is: A = lw.

Area of Home A: 62(94) = 5,828 square feet

Area of Home B: 90(112) = 10,080 square feet

Cost to build Home A/square foot: = $40.32

Cost to build Home B = 10,080($40.32) = $406,425.60

Income Properties

Example:

Bob, a local real estate investor, is interested in buying an income property that creates gross income in the amount of $270,500. He discovers that the operating costs of this property will equal 65% of the gross income. Ideally, he would like to acquire a 15% return. With his desire to have a 15% return, what is the most he can pay for the property?

Answer:

What do you know?

Gross income = $270,500

Operating costs = 65% of $270,500

Net income = Gross income – operating costs

Desired return= 15%

Most the investor can pay = x

Step #1:

Determine the dollar amount of the operating costs. Start off by converting the percentage to a decimal.

65% = .65

Operating costs = (.65)($270,500) = $175,825

Step #2:

Gross income – Operating costs = Net income

$270,500 - $175,825 = $94,675

Step #3:

The investor wants his net income to be 15% of what he pays for the property. Convert the percent to a decimal, and then determine the most he can pay.

15% = .15

$94,675 = (.15)(x)

$$\frac{\$94,675}{.15} = \frac{(.15)(x)}{.15}$$

$$\frac{\$94,675}{.15} = x$$

$631,167 (Rounded to the nearest dollar)

Depreciation

You may encounter "depreciation" problems on the exam, but those representing the straight-line method are the only ones you will probably see.

The formula for the straight-line method of depreciation:

$$\frac{replacement\ cost}{years\ of\ useful\ life} = \text{annual depreciation}$$

If the depreciation rate is not given, you can calculate it by dividing the total depreciation, which is 100%, by the useful life of the building.

For example, if a building has 25 years of useful life, then you will use this calculation:

$$\frac{100\%}{25} = 4\%$$

This means that the building has an annual depreciation rate of 4%.

Example:

It has been determined that the replacement cost of a 15-year-old building is $90,000. Since it has 35 years of useful life left, how much can be charged to annual depreciation?

What do you know?

Replacement cost = $90,000

Useful life = 35 years

Using the formula $\dfrac{replacement\ cost}{years\ of\ useful\ life}$ = annual depreciation, calculate annual depreciation.

$\dfrac{\$90,000}{35}$ = $2,571 (Rounded to the nearest dollar)

Example:

The annual depreciation of a building is $3,245. What is the total depreciation of a 19-year-old building?

annual depreciation x age of building = total depreciation

$3,245 x 19 = $61,655

Total depreciation = $61,655

Example:

The replacement cost of a building is $62,000. The total depreciation of said building is $19,354. What is the current value of the building?

replacement cost – depreciation = current value

$62,000 - $19,354 = $42,646

Current value of the building = $42,646

Summary

It is our hope that this Real Estate Math review has helped reinforce your knowledge of the topics you will most likely see on the math section of the Real Estate Exam. For those of you who feel like you could use a bit more of a refresher, feel free to take the included practice exams over and over until you feel confident that you can triumphantly complete the Real Estate Exam. Good luck!

Real Estate Glossary

>A

abandonment giving up the right to possess a property, building or real estate area through non-use and intention.

abstract of title the background of a property listing legal transactions and information.

abutting sitting next to another property.

acceleration clause an addendum that forces the borrower to repay the entire loan upon the lender's insistence for specific reasons listed in the clause.

acceptance agreement to an offer.

accretion increase of the amount of land by natural deposits of soil on onto the property.

accrued depreciation the total loss of value on the property.

accrued items the additional costs still outstanding at the close of the real estate deal, such as interest, insurance, HOA fees or taxes.

acknowledgement agreement to fulfill admitted responsibility.

acre a section of land that is 4,840 square yards or 43,560 square feet in area.

actual eviction a step-by-step procedure to remove renters from property.

actual notice specific information given to a party, such as a tenant, landlord, buyer or seller.

addendum a clause that provides more specific information to clarify a contract.

adjacent property or buildings next to each other but might not touch each other.

adjoining property or buildings next to each other that do touch each other.

adjustable rate mortgage (ARM) a loan rate that changes throughout the period of the loan. Sometimes called a variable rate or flexible rate.

adjusted basis the final cost of a property after improvements are added and deductions or reduced value are subtracted.

adjustment date the date agreed upon by the buyer and seller for financial changes.

administrator a court-appointed individual who executes a person's estate if there is not a will.

ad valorem **tax** property tax on the current value of the land.

adverse possession the ways by which a person may acquire property, such as through purchase, inheritance or other methods, including without payment as in a squatter.

affidavit a sworn promise before a person in authority.

agency a professional company that can act on behalf of another, such as a real estate agency or a title agency.

agent a professional individual who can act on behalf of another, such as a real estate agent or a title agent.

agreement of sale a contract between two parties to buy/sell property, usually over time.

air rights the right to air space above a property, separate from the property land itself.

alienation placement of ownership of property from one person/company to another person/company.

alienation clause an addendum to the mortgage contract that keeps the borrower from reselling the property without paying the lender.

allodial system a national system overseen by law that monitors property ownership.

amenities "extras" on a property that make it worth more or more attractive to buyers. Location or kitchen upgrades are two examples of amenities.

amortization paying off the principal and interest on a debt with equal payments until the debt is repaid.

amortization schedule the time frame set up over which the principal and interest of the debt is repaid.

amortize to pay off the principle and interest on a loan.

annual percentage rate (APR) the percentage above the principal added onto the loan over 12 months. It includes additional costs, such as closing costs and fees, and not just interest rates.

anti-deficiency law a statute that stops the lender from pursuing the buyer for a loss on a property after a foreclosure sale.

antitrust laws national laws that encourage free market trade and practices and prohibit the restriction of such.

apportionments the division of costs, such as fees and HOA responsibilities, between the seller and purchaser.

appraisal assessing the worth of land or property by a professional, qualified person who is usually licensed.

appraised value the worth of the land or property as determined by the licensed professional.

appraiser a professional, qualified person so licensed by the state to determine the value of land or property.

appreciation growth in the worth of real estate.

appurtenance an attachment to land or edifices that now conveys with the property.

arbitration dispute resolution through the use of a third party.

ARELLO an online company that encourages the cooperation of decision makers in the real estate business.

assessed value the tax-related value put on a property.

assessment the placement of tax-related value on a property.

assessor a professional who determines the tax-related value of a property.

asset something of value that belongs to a person, such as cash, property, bonds, etc.

assignment the transfer of a mortgage from one agency to another.

assumption of mortgage the process of the buyer taking over the seller's mortgage.

attachment placing a legal hold on a property to pay for a judgment.

attest to agree to the truth of a document by signing it.

attorney-in-fact a person who acts as a legal representative for another; does not need to be a professional lawyer.

avulsion transfer of land because water, such as a stream or brook, changes course.

>B

balloon mortgage a mortgage with small payments due for a specified period, such as three to five years with a lump sum or balloon due at the end of the mortgage.

balloon payment the lump payment at the end of a balloon mortgage.

bankruptcy the legal discharge of most debts through the courts.

bargain and sale deed a document transferring property from seller to buyer without guaranteeing the validity of the transfer.

baseline a line in surveying that runs east to west and acts a point of reference for corresponding lines that run north to south.

benchmark a fixed point of reference by which elevation is marked.

beneficiary the recipient of the profits that occur as a result of someone else's actions

bequest similar to an inheritance, a transfer of personal property through a will.

betterment an upgrade to property.

bilateral contract a contract, such as a rent agreement, when both parties agree to comply with or not comply with certain terms.

bill of sale a legal paper that transfers ownership of property from one person (company) to another.

binder money paid to hold a property for set terms.

biweekly mortgage payments made on real estate every two weeks as opposed to once a month. In some cases, this reduces the time needed to pay off the loan.

blanket mortgage a mortgage owned by the same person on at least two properties.

blockbusting an illegal process that involves scaring residents of an area into selling their property at reduced prices so that an agent can take advantage of them.

bona fide legal adjective that describes faithful, trustworthy actions or people.

bond a type of insurance money that protects a professional against loss.

boot a sum of cash included in a buyer/seller agreement to even out exchange.

branch office a satellite or another office that is at separate place from headquarters.

breach of contract breaking a binding agreement illegally.

broker professional or entity that is qualified through classes and licensed to buy or sell property.

brokerage a firm that employs one or more real estate professionals; real estate company.

broker's price opinion (BPO) an estimate on the worth of real estate by a professional in the industry.

building code state and local legislation that regulates new edifices or structural changes or existing ones.

building line an invisible boundary line around the property. The building must stay within this boundary.

building restrictions state, local and neighborhood guidelines or constraints that guide how it is built or determine property use.

bundle of rights privileges associated with property ownership, such as residency or use.

buy down payment by the buyer of added fees or points to the seller or lender for a lower interest rate.

buyer's broker a real estate professional who searches for a property and conducts negotiations in order to purchase the property.

bylaws procedural guidelines used to conduct business or meetings at an organization like a homeowners association.

>C

cancellation clause a section in a contract that permits parties to nullify the obligations of the contract.

canvassing surveying or soliciting an area to see if people are interested in selling their home.

cap the maximum increase in interest for a mortgage with changing rates.

capital funds used to generate more money.

capital expenditure money spent to improve the value of real estate.

capital gains tax taxation on the proceeds from a property sale.

capitalization the total yearly potential earnings on a property, such as a rental.

capitalization rate a percentage that can be used to compare investment opportunities. This is determined by dividing the yearly capitalization by the cost of the property.

cash flow the final amount of income generated from a rental property after income and expenses.

caveat emptor Latin expression meaning "let the buyer beware." Serves as a warning to the buyer.

CC&R covenants, conditions and restrictions – the bylaws for a group of homeowners.

certificate of discharge an IRS document that enables the government to waive taxes on a property.

certificate of eligibility formal document from the Veterans Administration that proves the person qualifies for a VA loan.

certificate of reasonable value (CRV) the maximum value permitted for a VA mortgage.

certificate of sale permits the buyer to receive the title for the purchase of the property.

certificate of title an official decision on the ownership, status or availability of a piece of real estate through public documents.

chain of title the legal document that tells the history of a piece of real estate.

chattel any property someone owns except real estate.

chattel mortgage the use of personal property as security for debt repayment.

city an incorporated group of residences larger than a town or village.

clear title a document of ownership that is completely valid.

closing the final legal transfer of property ownership through the signing of official papers.

closing costs the monies associated with the sale of property, such as inspection fees.

closing date the actual date the property will transfer from the buyer to the seller.

closing statement a final summary of all costs involved in the sale of real estate.

cloud on the title a questionable title as to the availability for sale.

clustering a group of residential buildings used to maximize land use.

codicil an addendum to a will that explains additions or deletions to the document.

coinsurance clause a clause in an insurance policy that divides financial responsibility for a loss between at least two parties.

collateral something of value that promises the repayment of a loan.

collection efforts to acquire delinquent rent or mortgage payments.

color of title a title that is invalid although it seemed to be valid initially.

commercial property real estate set aside for business use.

commingling combining the funds of two parties into one account

commission the payment that a broker or real estate agent receives for the sale of a property, usually a percentage of the sale price.

commitment letter a document from the mortgage company that informs the borrower regarding loan approval and the terms of said approval.

common areas regions of a neighborhood or apartment complex that all residents share, such as a pool, playground or parking lot.

common law originating in England, law based in part on traditions and in part on the courts.

community property real estate and chattel shared by 2 parties, usually husband and wife.

comparable sales used to help determine current market value, the latest sales of similar properties in the area are comparable sales

comparative market analysis (CMA) assessing the worth of real estate through the value of similar pieces of real estate in the area. See comparable sales.

competent parties those who can legally sign a contract.

condemnation taking over ownership of a property, usually by the government, and paying the owner for the real estate.

condominium individual residences in a building or area with common areas shared jointly by all residents.

condominium conversion the transfer in ownership in a condominium from one owner to many for each residence.

conformity the belief that similar pieces of real estate will retain their worth.

consideration a legal enticement that attracts the buyer to sign the contract.

construction mortgage a two-part loan – first, to pay for construction costs and next to pay for the home. Usually the borrower pays interest only payments until the home is finished when the mortgage transitions into a regular loan.

constructive eviction when a tenant moves out of a residence because of the poor quality of the residence without being liable for rent.

constructive notice public record and therefore common information to all.

contingency certain requirements that must be met to fulfill the contract, such as sale of the buyer's home so that he can afford the new residence

contract a legal arrangement between two legal parties that establishes certain conditions that will happen.

contract for deed a deferment of the price of the property for a specific time frame.

conventional loan financing to obtain a piece of property or real estate.

conversion option an agreement that the buyer can change an adjustable interest rate to a fixed rate. There is a cost associated with this option.

convertible ARM an agreement that the buyer can change an adjustable interest rate to a fixed rate. There is a cost associated with this option.

conveyance the legal transfer of property from one party to another.

cooperative ownership in shares of a common residential building, similar to an apartment, which allows the owners to live there.

corporation a company acts as its own business with liability and management.

cost approach a way to assess real estate value by starting with the worth of the property, subtracting costs and adding improvements.

counteroffer saying no to a real estate offer and then suggesting a different offer.

covenant specifications included in the deed requiring obligations or restrictions on real estate use.

covenant of seisin a legal verification that the owner has the right to the property.

credit available financial backing for real estate that needs to be repaid in the future.

credit history a list of borrowers or lenders who have lent the individual money and a history of how they have fulfilled their financial obligations.

cul-de-sac a semi-private road with a circular type of dead-end, usually adds value in real estate.

curtesy a man's ownership of some or all of his spouse's property even if she will deny him such ownership.

curtilage the area in close proximity to a residence, including other buildings, but not including open lands away from the home.

>D

damages financial or other compensation to the hurt party for tangible or intangible losses.

datum a horizontal reference point used to make vertical measurements.

DBA "doing business as" – sometimes used as an "also known as" name for a company.

debt money or property that is owed to another and must be repaid.

debt service repayment over a specific time frame, usually of a mortgage, including interest and principal.

decedent a person who passed way, often used to discuss their estate, will, inheritance or other financial matters.

dedication a gift of property for the benefit of all and the receipt of land by authorities.

deed the official, written proof that transfers and verifies property ownership.

deed-in-lieu used instead of a foreclosure, the property owner returns the property deed back to the lender to avoid a public record of foreclosure in some cases.

deed of trust a type of mortgage used in some jurisdictions.

deed restriction part of the deed that prevents the owner from certain land uses.

default failure to make a loan payment within a certain time frame, usually within 30 days of the due date.

defeasance clause the legal option that the lender has to repossess delinquent payments or the property from the borrower in case of a default.

deficiency judgment a legal document ordering the collection of the difference between what a borrower owes to the bank and the sale price of a home.

delinquency late payment on a loan.

density zoning regulations that prohibit more than a certain number of homes in an area.

depreciation a reduction in the value of an asset because of financial, physical or use.

descent the passing down of property to an heir if the deceased person has not left specific provisions.

devise a gift of real estate to an heir through a will.

devisee the person who receives a gift of property from a will.

devisor the person who gives a gift of property to another through a will.

directional growth the direction in which a city is expanding.

discount point money paid to the mortgage holder to reduce the interest payment. The more money that is paid, the lower the interest will fall.

discount rate the interest rate that a bank will pay to the Federal Reserve to borrow cash for short-term loans.

dispossess legal process of eviction.

dominant estate (tenement) property that benefits from the shared use of land on a neighboring property.

dower a woman's ownership of some or all of her spouse's property even if his will denies her such ownership.

down payment cash, as part of the cost of real estate, paid separately from the financing.

dual agency a real estate agent or broker who acts on behalf of two or more parties in a sale.

due-on-sale clause requires the loan to be repaid to the lender when the real estate is sold.

duress a person feels threatened into doing something, such as selling property.

>E

earnest money money to prove the buyer's serious intent of purchasing the home.

easement an agreement that one person has the privilege of use of another's land.

easement by necessity the need to walk on someone else's property by necessity.

easement by prescription accepted use of property by another person that is unnecessary. This becomes legal when it occurs over a certain number of years, such as a short cut through a neighbor's yard.

easement in gross accepted use of property that remains with the individual and does not convey with the property. For example, when the home is sold to a different owner, the easements are not passed to the new owner.

economic life the length of time when real estate will continue to earn money.

effective age the age of the building based on the condition of the building.

emblements different types of farming crops considered part of property.

eminent domain the purchase of private property by the government for public purposes.

encroachment part of real estate that crosses property boundaries onto another's property.

encumbrance assessments against a property, such as delinquent HOA fees, any mortgages or easements that impact the value.

equitable title the right someone who has to a property when they commit to buy it although the deal is not yet finalized.

equity the worth of the property above the mortgage or other debts on the property.

equity of redemption the reclaiming of real estate by the mortgage holder because of foreclosure.

erosion slow wearing away of land by natural elements, such as flooding.

escalation clause passing on increased expenses to tenants, such as fuel or HOA fees.

escheat real estate goes to the state if a person dies without a will and without any heirs.

escrow money or something of value held in trust by a third party until the completion of a specific transaction.

escrow account monies collected from the buyer that the lender holds in reserve to pay property taxes and homeowner's insurance.

escrow analysis a yearly review that assesses the monies collected in escrow to ensure that the amount is correct. It may be increased or decreased at that time to reconcile the account.

escrow disbursements the use of the escrow account to pay taxes, insurances and expenses.

estate all of a person's property.

estate for years time frame during which a person accesses land or property.

estate tax the tax on the worth of the assets when a person dies. A certain portion of the estate is exempt.

estoppel written confirmation that the borrower signs stating that the mortgage amount is correct.

et al. Latin for "and others"; used to refer to property ownership by several people, "Jane Doe, et. al."

et ux. Latin for "and wife."

et vir. Latin for "and husband."

eviction the process by which a person is legally removed from a property.

evidence of title official paperwork that proves that someone owns the property.

examination of title history of the title although not as complete or detailed as a title search.

exchange similar business or investment properties that can be traded tax-free per IRS Code 1031.

exclusive agency listing a binding legal agreement that gives a single broker permission to sell real estate for a certain time frame.

exclusive right to sell a binding legal agreement that gives the real estate agent the right to collect the commission if anyone else sells the property during the specified time frame.

exculpatory clause permits the borrower to give back the real estate to the lien holder without personal responsibility to repay the mortgage.

execution when a creditor wants to enforce the payment of the debt, he will require the debtor to turn over the property.

executor/executrix the person established by the deceased to perform estate duties. Executrix is a female who performs these duties.

executory contract a legal agreement that is awaiting action by at least one party for completion.

executed contract a completed contract.

express contract a contract that details all aspects, such as offer, acceptance and consideration.

extension agreement a mutual decision to lengthen the time frame for a contract.

external obsolescence a reduction in the worth of a specific home improvement because of something separate from the real estate that decreases the worth of the home.

>F

fair housing law a national statute that prohibits discrimination in any housing dealings because of race, color, sex, religion, family status, handicap or national origin.

fair market value what the property will sell for according to both buyer and seller.

Federal Housing Administration (FHA) a government agency that guarantees loans to make housing easier to obtain.

Federal National Mortgage Association (Fannie Mae) a federal organization that helps keep the home loan market solvent by purchasing notes from bankers.

Federal Reserve System the government banking system that oversees banks, offers services and sets national economic policy.

fee simple full and complete ownership of real estate.

FHA-insured loan a mortgage that is backed by the government through the FHA. VA loans are also backed by the government.

fiduciary relationship a person who acts on another's behalf in business or general matters.

finder's fee money that the realtor pays to a third party who finds a buyer; usually illegal.

first mortgage the first loan taken out on a home, usually in chronological order, but not always.

fixed-rate loan a loan where the interest rate remains the same throughout the loan term.

fixture personal property affixed to the building that conveys with the building when it is sold.

foreclosure the process by which a buyer loses the property because of failure to pay the debt, which results in the public sale of the real estate in order to pay as much of the debt as possible.

forfeiture seizure of property because of criminal actions or failure to fulfill a contract.

franchise when a business owner pays to use a company name in return for company backing, such as member brokerages.

fraud deceptive actions intended to mislead another person and harm them

freehold estate continued ownership or stake in a property as compared to a temporary stake or a lease.

front foot the measurement at the front of the home nearest the street; used to compare home value especially on the same street.

functional obsolescence the decrease in worth on the real estate except those caused by wear and tear.

future interest a right to real estate that will occur in the future.

>G

general agent someone who can do any job duties related to the business on behalf of the principal. A real estate agent acts as a special agent.

general lien a mortgage that covers more than one property owned by the same person.

general warranty deed a guarantee that the title is free and clear of other claims against it for the protection of the buyer.

government-backed mortgage a loan that is backed by the federal government as contrasted with a conventional loan.

Government National Mortgage Association (Ginnie Mae) a federal agency that supplies funding for government loans.

government survey system a process of dividing land into rectangle sections in order to set area boundaries.

graduated lease a rental agreement that permits periodic adjustments in rental price increases.

grant the exchanging of real estate to another individual through a deed.

grant deed the legal document used to transfer real estate to another.

grantee the person who receives the real estate; buyer.

grantor the person who sells the real estate.

gross income all financial gains received for real estate before any losses or expenses on the property.

gross income multiplier (also **gross rent multiplier**) a way to assess the profitability of property arrived at by dividing the total price paid by the monthly rental rate.

gross lease a rental agreement when the landlord pays all costs associated with the property, including HOA fees, repairs, taxes, and more.

ground lease a lease of land only, not of buildings.

guaranteed sale plan a contract between the seller and the real estate agent/broker. The broker promises to buy the property for predetermined terms if the property does not sell by a certain date.

guardian a person who the court deems legally responsible for someone who is incapable of managing his affairs.

>H

habendum clause "to have and to hold" that specifies any restrictions on property; fee simple absolute.

hamlet a small, populated area; municipality.

heir someone who receives property, often through a will after a death.

hereditament anything either tangible or intangible given through a will.

highest and best use the most productive use of real estate that will provide the greatest financial return over a specified period of time.

holdover tenancy a renter who stays on the property when the lease ends.

holographic will a handwritten will signed by the person who makes the will; does not need a notary or witness.

home equity conversion mortgage (HECM) reverse mortgage or when a lender makes payments, usually monthly, to a homeowner.

home equity line of credit a loan available to homeowners based on the equity in the home, similar to a credit card.

home inspection a professional assessment of the real estate that closely examines the property.

homeowners association (HOA) a corporation or private party formed by a real estate developer an designed to market, manage or sell homes in a subdivision area.

homeowner's insurance an insurance policy that covers the property and contents against all types of natural and other damages, includes liability.

homeowner's warranty insurance coverage that protects the buyer against any defects in the residence.

homestead permitted by some states, protects a residence against lawsuits or judgments up to certain limits.

Housing Urban and Development Department (HUD) federal agency that regulates some aspects of the housing industry.

hypothecate a promise of something as pledge for a loan without physically relinquishing that item. Most homeowners live in their primary residence through this method unless they own the residence free and clear.

>I

implied contract an informal contract, not in writing, yet enforceable by the courts.

improvement work done on land or property that increases worth, additions or upgrades that are more consequential than repairs.

income capitalization approach a specific formula used to assess the income-producing worth of a property.

income property real estate that earns money for the owner.

incorporeal right intangible rights associated with real estate, such as easements and future income.

indemnify to insure against loss.

independent contractor the employment status of most real estate agents; those who work independently and do not have an employer/employee relationship.

index an assessment of the current financial atmosphere by the government; used to adjust prices.

industrial property real estate used for nonresidential but business purposes, such as a warehouse or manufacturing property.

inflation an increase in overall costs and expenses that results in a decrease in what money will buy.

initial interest rate the first or starting rate for an adjustable mortgage.

installment a scheduled payment toward the reduction of debt, such as a mortgage.

installment contract a binding, legal, written agreement that sets a schedule for the loan payments.

installment loan repaid in periodic payments at a set schedule; sometimes secured by personal property.

installment sale payments made to a seller over a longer period of time in order to defer taxes.

insurance money paid to an indemnity holder to reduce the expenses associated with the specific emergency being insured, such as flooding or earthquakes.

insurance binder temporary proof of insurance until the permanent paperwork is completed.

insured mortgage financial backing for a loan that protects the lender against default, sometimes called PMI.

interest a legal right to real estate or other property; the amount a lender charges a borrower for the loan above the principal, usually specified as a percentage.

interest accrual rate how often the interest accrues, such as daily, weekly or monthly, until it is paid to the lender.

interest rate the amount a lender charges a borrower for the loan above the principal, usually specified as a percentage.

interest rate buy down plan using money from a still uncompleted home sale to reduce the interest rate and the monthly costs to the buyer.

interest rate ceiling the maximum percentage rate cap on an adjustable rate mortgage.

interest rate floor the lowest percentage rate minimum on an adjustable rate mortgage.

interim financing a transitional loan to bridge the time frame until the buyer can obtain permanent financing, for example a construction loan.

intestate without a legal will or without any will at all.

invalid not legally enforceable, such as a will or a contract.

investment property real estate purchased for the purpose of generating income.

>J

joint tenancy more than one individual who owns property in common, usually related individuals.

joint venture more than one entity who works toward the same professional goal, usually a temporary arrangement for a specific purpose.

judgment the court order that sets the amount one person or entity owes another in the event of a default, such as a loan or an eviction.

judgment lien a lender's right to claim the property of the borrower because of a judgment.

judicial foreclosure court order to force the sale of real estate to pay off debt. The satisfaction of debts will stop foreclosure.

jumbo loan a property loan above the normal limits.

junior mortgage a loan that will only be satisfied after the first mortgage.

>L

laches the delay of the time during which a legal claim can be enforced.

land solid real estate, separate from water or air.

landlocked property that is not accessible to public roads except through a neighboring property.

lease a legal contact that lasts for a specific period during which the owner allows the renter to possess the property.

leased fee a restriction on property because of a rental/lease agreement.

lease option the renter can decide to buy the property under certain conditions.

leasehold property subject to a long-term rental agreement.

legal description authoritative confirmation of a property through written, technical means.

lessee tenant of real estate property.

lessor landlord of real estate property.

leverage the mortgage used to purchase a home or business.

levy a legal order of payment of any money due.

license legal permission, such as the temporary use of property.

lien financial assessment against real estate that must be paid when the land is sold.

life estate a lifelong interest in a specific real estate that ends when the owner dies.

life tenant someone who can stay on the real estate property until their death.

liquidity the availability of cash when using assets, such as property or real estate.

lis pendens Latin for "suit pending." Notice of possible restrictions on title when a lawsuit is filed.

listing agreement a contract between a real estate agent and client that pays commission to the agent no matter how the buyer finds the property.

listing broker the real estate agent who lists the property.

littoral rights the shore land next to an ocean or very large water body that the property owner has rights to.

loan borrowing money from another entity.

loan officer a representative for the lender or for the borrower to the lender who may also look for loans.

lock-in the borrower pays a fee to guarantee a certain interest rate for a specific time period, especially if the borrower thinks the interest rates will rise.

lock-in period the time frame of the lock-in, such as 90 days.

lot and block description a legal process of finding real estate based on its lot and block identification within the housing area.

>M

management agreement a legal agreement between an owner and a property manager for a percentage of the rental generated.

margin a flat percentage to adjust interest rates up or down according to the index used in adjustable rate mortgages.

market data approach a comparison of recent property sales to assess real estate worth.

market value in real estate, price range between the maximum purchase price and minimum purchase price.

marketable title a free-and-clear title.

mechanic's lien a hold on the construction and on the real estate that guarantees payment for the work done on the property.

metes and bounds specific description of the land that identifies all boundaries of the real estate.

mill one-tenth of a penny; used for taxation.

minor a person who is not of legal age to make a binding decision.

misrepresentation a misleading verbalization even if unintended.

modification a legal alteration to a contract.

money judgment a court order that orders a financial payment.

month-to-month tenancy a rental agreement that can be extended or cancelled each month.

monument a landmark or immovable object used to decide the land locations.

mortgage a loan on property that uses the property itself as security for the repayment of the property.

mortgage banker a bank that finances loans for others, which are then sometimes purchased by federal agencies.

mortgage broker an agency that researches and finds loans for others but does not finance them.

mortgage lien the financing on a piece of real estate that obligates the buyer to the holder.

mortgagee the person/agency who lends money in a real estate transaction.

mortgagor the person/agency who borrows money in a real estate transaction.

multi-dwelling units a building, such as an apartment complex, that has separate living units but only one property loan.

multiple-listing system (MLS-also multiple-listing service) a group of real estate agents that lists all the available properties for sale, which gives a buyer a wide range of choices.

mutual rescission an agreement to void a contract by all involved parties.

>N

negative amortization a deferment of interest payments on a loan, which is added on to the principal and results in an eventual increase in the payments over time and a loss of value on the home.

net income when all bills have been paid, the earnings that remain.

net lease the renter, as opposed to the landlord, pays costs, such as HOA fees, repairs and upkeep.

net listing any funds above the original price of the property that are paid to the real estate agent, illegal in some places.

net worth the positive, monetary difference between the value of assets and liabilities.

no cash-out refinance sometimes called a "rate and term refinance," the borrower receives no cash, but the money is used to recalculate the loan and related costs.

non-conforming use a code violation related to property use that is permitted because it was "grandfathered in." In other words, the property owner began the questionable property use before the zoning ordinance took effect.

nonliquid asset something of worth that is difficult to convert to cash.

notarize to witness the veracity of a signature.

notary public a person with the legal and official authority to witness the veracity of a signature.

note the written loan that admits debt and promises repayment.

note rate the interest rate on a loan or mortgage.

notice of default official notification that the borrower has defaulted and that the lender can take additional legal remedies.

novation the substitution of one party for another party in a contract.

>O

obligee a person requesting a certain duty in their favor.

obligor a person required to perform a certain duty, often under bond.

obsolescence a decrease in worth because of outdated design or construction, such as a home without a dishwasher or cable hook-up.

offer a suggestion or expression of desire to buy or sell real estate.

offer and acceptance the suggestion or expression of desire to buy or sell real estate and the acceptance of the offer by the other party.

open-end mortgage a loan with smaller amount than the maximum funds that a borrower can access from the lender.

open listing more than one real estate agent can list the property; the first to close the sale is the one who receives payment.

opinion of title legal authentication that the title is clear.

option an agreement that allows a buyer to purchase a property at a specific price if done so within a specific time period.

optionee the person who has available choices.

optionor the person who gives or sells the available choices.

ordinance a statute or legislation related to property use.

original principal balance the loan amount before the first payment is made.

origination fee fees assessed to the borrower that cover loan expenses related to the title, appraisal and credit checks.

owner financing the seller provides the buyer with the loan; the buyer does not go through a bank.

ownership possession of property.

>P

package mortgage a combination loan that covers both the residence and the land.

parcel a section of real estate under the person who owns it.

participation mortgage a loan that permits the holder to receive a portion of the profits from the property.

partition equal division of property between all owners.

partnership business relationship between two or more parties subject to debt and tax laws.

party wall divides two properties with ownership rights for both users.

payee the seller who receives money or something of value.

payor the buyer who gives the payee money or something of value.

percentage lease a rental payment determined by sales volume of the renter with a minimum rental amount.

periodic estate a rental agreement that goes for a specific time frame, such as month-to-month.

personal property (hereditaments) anything either tangible or intangible given through a will.

physical deterioration decrease in property worth because of normal wear, failure to repair, or things breaking .

PITI principal, interest, taxes and insurance payment; usually the total of all payments due on the property.

planned unit development (PUD) zoning permission to design a subdivision with flexibility and creativity.

plat description of a section of land that provides detailed information about the area.

plat book public information with the description of a section of land that provides detailed information about the area.

plat number the number associated with each lot in a plat.

plottage combining small sections of real estate into a larger parcel.

PMI private mortgage insurance; used to cover the default of the loan.

point one percent of the loan amount; monies paid to entice a lender to lend money to the borrower, sometimes used in exchange for a reduction in the interest rate on the loan.

point of beginning the exact same starting and ending point on a land survey as the survey borders and encloses the property.

police power the government's ability to address the overall well-being of the community.

power of attorney the legal right for one person to perform duties for another either some or all of the time.

preapproval qualifying a buyer prior to purchase of the home.

prepayment paying costs or monies due early, sometimes as escrow funds.

prepayment penalty the expenses associated with early pay-off of a loan.

prequalification preapproval, sometimes in writing, before the buyer can purchase the home.

prescription receiving the right to a property through common use, such as a squatter, or adverse possession.

primary mortgage market the original buyer of a loan, such as a bank or savings and loan, which may then be sold on the secondary mortgage market for a profit.

prime rate the lowest available interest rate a lending institution charges on short-term loans to businesses.

principal the face value of a loan or mortgage, separate from the interest, taxes and insurance.

principal meridian an imaginary north/south line used as a reference point in surveying to describe land.

probate to confirm the authenticity of a will.

procuring cause a method of deciding if the real estate agent earned a commission, legal expression that means the goal was realized through the actions.

promissory note a written statement of a promise to pay.

property management oversight of different aspects of property, such as collecting payments, upkeep, leasing units, cleaning units.

property tax real estate tax based on worth that is collected by the government.

prorate to equally divide a financial assessment between a buyer and a seller, for example as HOA fees or property taxes.

pur autre vie "For the life of another," use of property that one individual gives another, as long as the third person is alive.

purchase agreement also called contract of sale or agreement of sale; a written contract between a buyer and seller.

purchase money mortgage a mortgage loan that the purchaser gives the seller as partial payment for property.

>Q

qualifying ratios the ratio of the buyer's debt when compared to the buyer's income, which must be below a certain percentage for a lending institution to offer the loan.

quitclaim deed a release of rights in a property without confirming the validity or the rights of the person who keeps the deed.

>R

range a six-mile wide area of land. Using the rectangular survey system, it is labeled east or west.

ready, willing, and able a buyer who is ready to buy and follows through with the requirements needed to close the sale.

real estate land, the air above it, the ground under it and any buildings.

real estate agent a person who acts on the behalf of another to make a transaction with a third party.

real estate board a group of professional agents who belong to the National Association of Realtors.

real estate broker a person who acts on the behalf of another to make a transaction with a third party.

Real Estate Settlement Procedures Act (RESPA) a law that informs buyers of their rights by requiring the lender to give updated information to the borrower throughout the home buying process.

real property real estate, physical land and structures on the land.

realtor a professional real estate agent.

recording the official documentation related to a change in property title, such as a sale or transfer.

rectangular survey system a survey method of dividing land into squares and grids.

redemption period a time frame when an owner can buy back real estate that was foreclosed.

redlining illegal action of refusing to lend money to an individual in a lower socio-economic area without considering the circumstances of the individual.

refinance transaction obtaining a new loan on real estate and paying off the first loan using the same real estate as collateral.

Regulation Z federal requirement that a lender must disclose all terms of a loan, including the APR.

release clause a section in a contract that allows the buyer to pay off part of the loan, which then frees a piece of the real estate from the loan.

remainder estate the real estate that passes to another individual when the first individual's rights in the real estate end.

remainderman the individual who real estate goes to when a life tenant dies.

remaining balance the amount still left to pay on a loan.

remaining term the length of time still left to pay on a loan.

rent payment for temporary use of property; lease.

replacement cost the amount of money needed to replicate an edifice so that it can fulfill previous functions.

reproduction cost the amount of money needed for an exact replica of an edifice.

rescission the negating of a contract so that it is no longer in effect.

restriction (restrict covenant) prevents the real estate from being used in certain manners, either in the deed or through local laws.

reversion the landlord's right to take possession of rental property when the rental agreement ends.

reversionary interest the interest the remainderman has in the ownership of the real estate as it passes to them when a life tenant dies.

reverse annuity mortgage a property loan used for a person with high equity when the lender makes yearly payments to the homeowner.

revision alteration or change (e.g. contract).

right of egress (or ingress) the right to leave real estate; the right to go to real estate.

right of first refusal the option an individual or entity has to fulfill a legal agreement before another person or entity meets those obligations.

right of redemption the owner's privilege to take possession of real estate when the financial obligations of the loan have been met even during the process of foreclosure.

right of survivorship the remaining survivor's right to take over the interest of the deceased survivor.

riparian rights water rights in close proximity to a person's real estate.

>S

safety clause an extender clause or protection clause that gives the broker a commission if a buyer who sees the home returns later to close the sale.

sale-leaseback the sale of the real estate to a new owner and the new owner rents the real estate back to the original owner.

sales contract a legal agreement between a buyer and seller to finalize a sale.

salesperson a professional and licensed real estate agent or broker.

salvage value used to determine depreciation; the worth of a property or asset when its service is over.

satisfaction a document that verifies and confirms the mortgage payoff.

second mortgage a mortgage obtained after the first mortgage used for a down payment, refinancing or cash.

section a unit of measurement in the government rectangular system, one-square mile.

secured loan a loan that uses collateral in the case of default.

security the real estate used as collateral in case of default when money is borrowed.

seisin the owner who holds the title to the property free and clear.

selling broker the real estate agent who finds a buyer for the property.

separate property property that belongs to only one spouse as opposed to both spouses.

servient tenement property that gives shared use of land to a neighboring property for their good.

setback a boundary away from the edge of the property that must remain free of buildings.

settlement statement (HUD-1) a full accounting of all the monetary transactions that occur in a property sale.

severalty independent interest of real estate by a person.

special assessment a financial levy against real estate to pay for something of benefit to that real estate.

special warranty deed a deed that pertains only to the title under the person issuing it, not to any title issues from previous title holders.

specific lien a mortgage or lien against only a specified part of the real estate.

specific performance mandate by the court that the party in a contract fulfill their duties.

standard payment calculation a process of calculating monthly equal payments needed to pay the balance owed on a mortgage at the present interest rate.

statute of frauds legal necessity for real estate contracts to be written.

statute of limitations a time period after which someone cannot file a law suit.

statutory lien a legal obligation on the property, such as taxes.

steering illegal action when only certain racial or cultural groups are shown a property.

straight-line depreciation the total depreciation divided by the number of years of depreciation.

subdivision a division of land into lots upon which homes are built.

sublet to rent from another renter.

subordinate a lesser priority, as in a subordinate mortgage that would be paid off only if the first mortgage was satisfied in a foreclosure.

substitution replacing the market worth of one piece of real estate for another piece of real estate, usually viewed as indifferent by buyers.

subrogation the legal substitution of one individual for another individual, with all rights passing onto the new party.

suit for possession eviction lawsuit after a break of contract by a renter.

suit for specific performance a lawsuit filed by the buyer for breach of contract in property sale. The court can either require the seller to pay damages and expenses or complete the sale.

survey the boundaries of a parcel of real estate; a map of the property surveyed.

syndicate a group of people or entities who join resources to invest in real estate.

>T

tax deed a legal document that places a claim on real estate because of owed taxes.

tax lien a hold placed on real estate because of owed taxes prior to filing the tax deed.

tax rate the rate at which an individual property is taxed

tax sale the sale of real estate because taxes have not been paid.

tenancy at sufferance a renter who can no longer legally remain on the property because the lease has ended.

tenancy at will an agreement the owner provides to the renter that ends if and when the landlord decides to end it. The renter can also terminate the lease.

tenancy by the entirety equal rights to property shared between spouses, the real estate passes to the surviving spouse upon death of a spouse.

tenancy in common equal rights to property shared between individuals without surviving rights but determined through a will upon one party's death.

tenant renter who pays the landlord a fee for property use.

tenement a fixture that remains as part of the land.

testate a person who dies with a legal will in place.

"time is of the essence" following a contract according to time specifications to prevent delays in fulfilling the contract.

time sharing a piece of real estate owned by more than one person; each person has the right to a specific time at the property.

title legal proof and verification of property ownership.

title insurance insurance that covers the owner from problems with the title.

title search scrutiny of legal records to review the rights to and encumbrances against real estate.

Torrens system a short-cut type of title registration available in some jurisdictions without going through the lengthy process of a title search.

township a section of land in the government rectangular survey system; six square miles.

trade fixtures fixtures, such as furniture and appliances, used in a specific business; may convey with the property upon the expiration of the lease.

trust a holding that transfers the real estate to the trustee for the beneficiary.

trustee the person who keeps the real estate for the beneficiary.

Truth-in-Lending Law federal requirement that a lender must disclose all terms of a loan, including the APR.

>U

underwriting similar to insuring; validating the policy.

undivided interest shared rights and ownership of property among all owners.

unilateral contract one party has a duty to fulfill a certain responsibility in the contract but the other party does not.

unsecured loan a loan that uses no collateral but may be based on the borrower's credit worthiness.

useful life the period of time during which improvements will yield income.

usury charging a higher than maximum interest rate; illegal.

>V

VA-guaranteed loan a mortgage backed by the government agency, the Veterans Administration, which promises repayment to the lender for the main residence.

valid contract a legally binding contract that will hold up in a court of law.

valuation estimate of the price of real estate.

variance a deviation from zoning laws that permits the owner to violate zoning code.

vendee buyer of personal property.

vendor seller of personal property.

village a small grouping of residential properties and other buildings.

void contract a written agreement that cannot be enforced even when signed.

voidable contract a written agreement that becomes unenforceable after it is signed.

>W

waiver the abdication of certain rights.

warranty deed a legal right of protection against any type of claim.

waste specified abuse of mortgage or rental property that causes damages.

will legal document that transfers ownership of property to another upon the death of the person who writes the will.

wraparound mortgage a property loan that combines a first mortgage with a second mortgage at a higher loan amount and higher payment.

writ of execution an order that permits the court to sell the person's real estate, such as after a foreclosure.

>Z

zone a section regulated by local rules and conditions, such as a business zone that is prohibited from residential housing.

zoning ordinance a regulation that specifies the type of property use permitted in the area.

Real Estate Sales Exam I

1. A couple executes a sales contract on their home after several counter-offers with the buyer. In this case, the seller is:

a) the mortgagee

b) the grantor

c) the grantee

d) the mortgagor

2. The Cambridge family bought a house with a lot size of .25 of an acre. This is equivalent to:

a) 10,890 square feet

b) 43,560 square feet

c) 11,000 square feet

d) 5,250 square feet

3. A principal residence is sold for $527,000 by a couple in the 28% tax bracket. The home was originally purchased eight years ago for $313,000 and the family lived there the entire eight years. How much will be paid in capital gains?

a) $59,920

b) $32,100

c) $214,000

d) none of the above

4. An owner-occupied four-unit dwelling worth $525,000 generates $4,500 in income from three units and $150/month from the onsite laundry. If the current owner typically yields roughly 9% annually on his investment, what is the monthly effective gross amount?

a) $4,350

b) $6,000

c) $4.905

d) $4,650

5. A brother is moving out of the country and decides to sell his home to his sister for $275,000, making this the latest sale in that area. The sister decides to pay cash, as she says she will later get a home equity loan for $200,000. Recent sales comps of very similar homes had values of $325,000. Based on the information provided, what is best estimate of the market value of the subject property?

a) $325,000

b) $200,000

c) $275,000

d) not enough information provided

6. When can a landlord choose to not rent to someone with children?

a) Never, children are protected under Fair Housing

b) If the unit has evidence of lead paint

c) A lease of an owner-occupied three-family home

d) Someone on a temporary lease

7. A seller provides written permission allowing his listing broker (who has a fiduciary obligation to the seller) to work with the buyer. This relationship is known as:

a) Dual agency

b) Sub agency

c) Special agency

d) Implied agency

8. A homeowner purchased a home for $300,000 on a 30-year FHA loan with an interest rate of 4.25%. If he wants to do a cash out conventional refinance and eliminate the MIP, which of these loans is the largest he can get based on a future home value of $350,000?

a) $276,500

b) $310,000

c) $300,000

d) $240,000

9. A valid contract can be _____.

a: a verbal agreement
b: a 10-month lease

a) both a and b

b) b only

c) neither a nor b

d) a only

10. A brother is moving out of the country and decides to sell his home to his sister for $275,000, making this home the latest sale in that area. This sister puts 20% down and finances $220,000. Recent sales comps of very similar homes had values of $485,000. Based on the information provided, what is the market value?

a) $485,000

b) $220,000

c) $225,000

d) not enough information provided

11. Which best describes an example of emblements?

a) cherry tree, apple tree and tomato plants

b) cherry tree, apple tree and peach tree

c) tomato, lettuce and onion crops

d) none of these

12. Nine states recognize this system of property ownership where the husband and wife have equal interest in property acquired during marriage. This is_____.

a) common-law

b) community property

c) commingling

d) common title

13. A dad who owns his house free and clear decides to take out a HELOC and let his son make the payments. He also signs a quitclaim deed to transfer the home into his son's name. What clause might the lender enforce?

a) co-insurance clause

b) acceleration clause

c) due-on-sale clause

d) cancellation clause

14. A broker is given escrow money. He has until the end of what business day to deposit it in the correct account?

a) first

b) fifth

c) second

d) third

15. The Federal Home Loan Mortgage Corporation purchases primarily which loan types?

a) FHA

b) owner-financed notes

c) VA

d) conventional

16. Sally works for ABC Bank. Her job duties are to gather documents, review applications for accuracy, package the loan and take each file from pre-approval to closing. What is most likely her job title?

a) underwriter

b) processor

c) loan officer

d) appraiser

17. Which of the following does not lend money directly to borrowers?

a) insurance company

b) mortgage broker

c) cooperative bank

d) private lender

18. Jay decides that he's ready to move out of his parents' home and purchase his own home. He has a roommate who will be moving in so he would like at least a three-bedroom house. What should his first step be?

a) get prequalified by submitting a mortgage application

b) purchase new furniture

c) pick out a house

d) purchase a new car to go with the new house

19. Mike and Kathy have $30,000 or 10% down to purchase their first home. Their loan officer prequalifies them for several different loan types. They decide to go with the following scenario: purchase price: $300,000 with a loan amount of $300,000 and a $6,450 funding fee. What type of loan did they choose?

a) conventional

b) FHA

c) VA

d) negative amortization

20. A lender offers you a very low interest rate of 2.75% in exchange for part of your equity. What type of mortgage is this?

a) balloon

b) shared equity

c) wraparound mortgage

d) equity loan

21. Sellers Keith and Rita execute a standard purchase and sale agreement on November 1st. The contract also states that by Nov 15th their agent should receive a mortgage commitment letter. On November 14th, the buyers' agent sends over a letter that the buyers have been unable to secure financing. The buyers should expect:

a) their earnest money deposit back

b) to withdraw from the transaction

c) both a and b

d) a only

22. **House and Home Realty Brokerage leased a two-family residence for $1,500/month for each unit. Tenant 1 wrote a check to cover the first month's rent and deposit, and Tenant 2 paid by money order. Which is the best representation of what the brokerage must do?**

a) make and keep a copy of all funds collected from each tenant

b) nothing as long as the broker received the money that is sufficient

c) only copy the money order because a check is a legal record

d) tell the tenant to pay the owner directly

23. **Kimberly finds the home of her dreams, a cozy bungalow built in 1932. Her agent suspects that the home may have lead-based paint. Kimberly has how many days to test for lead-based paint?**

a) 5

b) 3

c) 7

d) 10

24. **The governor appoints nine members to the Texas Real Estate Commission. How many members are licensed brokers?**

a) 5

b) 9, all are licensed

c) 6

d) 4

25. **An appraisal is done on a unique property that sits on 42.5 acres. The approach the appraiser will more than likely use is _____.**

a) assumption

b) cost

c) income

d) market data

26. Jill secures a 15-year fixed conventional home loan. This loan was more than likely purchased by which investor?

a) FNMA

b) insurance company

c) an orb

d) GNMA

27. A homeowner has an existing mortgage balance of $120,000 with a mortgage payment of $1,375. He puts an ad in the newspaper to sell his home with owner financing where he will offer the buyer a new note based on a sales price of $258,000 at 5%. The buyer decides to use this financing to purchase the home. Based on the information given, what type of mortgage is this?

a) wraparound mortgage

b) junior mortgage

c) package mortgage

d) none of these

28. When determining whether a buyer is a good credit risk, the lender needs to evaluate:

a) borrower's credit, the borrower's ability to pay, and homeowner's age

b) ability to pay, property, borrower's 401K

c) borrower's credit, future expected value of the property, job stability

d) property, ability to pay, credit

29. When a buyer chooses to pay discount points, her goal is to receive_____.

a) cash back at closing

b) a lower interest rate

c) principal reduction

d) none of these

30. Kevin's sister decides she wants to purchase a home and needs to get prequalified. Kevin's sister's best friend James is a loan officer at the bank and tells him once the loan closes he will give him a referral fee. Which statement is true?

a) As long as James gives Kim the HUD information booklet within three days, he can pay a referral fee

b) James is protected under RESPA

c) James must disclose the referral amount on the GFE

d) Fees and kickbacks to individuals who do not provide a loan is prohibited

31. Members of the Texas Real Estate Commission serve a term of _____ years.

a) 6

b) 2

c) 7

D) 10

32. The purpose of which of the following laws is to prohibit discrimination in the sale of real property on the basis of only race?

a) Occupation Code 1101.558

b) TRELA

c) Federal Civil Rights Act of 1966

d) Federal Fair Housing Act of 1968

33. Another name for a HUD-1 is _____,

a) Good Faith Estimate

b) Uniform Settlement Statement

c) Truth-in-Lending document

d) Housing Uniform document

34. A homeowner attempts a refinance on his home only to find out that the home has two liens from the previous owner that were never paid off. Whom should he contact?

a) the title insurance company

b) the escrow office

c) the loan officer

d) a real estate attorney

35. All listing types below allow the sellers the right to sell their property on their own without paying a commission, EXCEPT_____.

a) an exclusive agency

b) open

c) exclusive right to sell

d) none of the above

36. Kurt receives a letter that an expressway is being built where his property sits. The state offers to purchase his home. What right is it (the state) exercising?

a) escheatment

b) foreclosure

c) adverse passion

d) eminent domain

37. A family leases a home with a pool. The contract states that the owner will pay property taxes and insurance, but the tenant must pay the pool and yard expenses. This is known as a _____ lease.

a) percentage

b) gross

c) net

d) month-to-month

38. Mr. Green has purchased new energy efficient windows, put weather stripping around the doors and replaced his old wall heater with a new central air and heat system. Mr. Green has _____ his home.

a) weatherized

b) energized

c) overhauled

d) redlined

39. The Edwards family is planning on buying a single family home for $319,750. They need to put down 20% in order to buy the home. How much money does the Edwards family need to put down to secure the house?

a. $68,010

b. $63,950

c. $63,600

d. $61,750

40. The total commission for the sale of a $449,000 property is 6%. The listing states that they will offer 3.5% to a co-broker who brings a buyer which ends in a successfully closed transaction. How much will the listing broker net after his sales agent, who is on a 45/55 (listing broker gets 55%) split, is paid?

a) $26,940

b) $15,715

c) $6,174

d) $11,225

41. Several first-time home buyers purchasing homes in a community redevelopment area noticed that they were not offered a fixed rate loan by the developer's lender. They were only offered adjustable rate mortgages. This is most likely an example of _____.

a) economic adjustments

b) redlining

c) conforming

d) steering

42. Susie is a licensed salesperson and would like to pursue her broker's license. How long must she work as a salesperson?

a) 3 years

b) 1 year

c) 6 months

d) 2 years

43. All are true except:

a) a licensee must be a Texas resident

b) a salesperson must take 210 hours of training

c) a licensee must be 21

d) a salesperson must take continuing education

44. FHA insured loans protect the:

a) lender

b) realtor

c) seller

d) buyer

45. The homestead is exempt from which of the following?

a) tax liens

b) homeowners' association lien

c) most creditors

d) mechanic's lien

46. A tenant signs a one-year lease where the owner allows him to occupy the property during this time. This is an example of _____.

a) fee simple

b) freehold estate

c) timeshare

d) non-freehold estate

47. What is placed outside the premises in Texas when the landlord wants the tenant to either comply with the terms of the lease or leave the premises?

a) Notice to Vacate

b) Notice to Quit

c) Notice of Compliance

d) Notice of Eviction

48. When someone who is upside down with their mortgage gets permission to sell their house for less than they owe, this process is known as:

a) short sale

b) foreclosure

c) deed restructure

d) deed-in-lieu of foreclosure

49. "OLD CAR" stands for:

a) obligation, litigation, disclosure, care, access, real estate

b) obedience, loyalty, dedication, confidentiality, accountability, realtor

c) obligation, license, disclosure, confidentiality, accountability, reasonable care

d) obedience, loyalty, disclosure, confidentiality, accountability, reasonable care

50. Mrs. Ramirez, the local real estate agent, made a profit of $19,500 off a house she just sold. The house closed for $325,000. What was Mrs. Ramirez's commission rate for the sale?
a. 11%

b. 8%

c. 6%

d. 15%

51. A broker's license can be revoked if he:

a) fails to return deposit funds to client when requested

b) commingles business and personal funds

c) violates TRELA

d) any of the above

52. A person dies leaving no will and no heirs. The decedent's property would transfer by:

a) adverse possession

b) state

c) escheat

d) laws of descent

53. Describe the ownership of a property if four cousins, Keenan, Kelly, Shon, and Marcia are joint tenants and Marcia sells her interest to her cousin Michael. The new deed will read:

a) tenants in common with Keenan, Kelly and Shon

b) tenants in will

c) joints tenant Keenan, Kelly and Shon

d) Marcia is not allowed to sell her interest

54. A transaction where the seller agrees to finance the loan of the buyer is called:

a) hard money loan

b) blanket mortgage

c) conventional loan

d) purchase money mortgage

55. A 2,980 square foot home sells for $328,000. If it sits on an acre lot, what is the price/ square foot the home sold for?

a) $94

b) $110

c) $116

d) $154

56. A lot recently sold for $198,000. It is 378' x 296.' What was the cost/acre?

a) $67,074

b) $70,774

c) $77,774

d) $77,085

57. If Michelle sells her home, and then remains on the property by becoming a tenant of the new landlord, this is known as:

a) testate

b) wraparound mortgage

c) sale leaseback

d) freehold

58. A homeowner puts a $104,250 down payment on a $417,000 home. What percentage is the down payment?

a) 25%

b) 18%

c) 20%

d) 30%

59. What happens if a subpoena issued by the Texas Real Estate Commission (TREC) is ignored?

a) the matter goes to district court

b) the broker is audited

c) a and b

d) nothing

60. An investor gets a 30-year loan due in 15 years. This is a:

a) VA loan

b) package mortgage

c) balloon mortgage

d) open-end mortgage

61. In order for Farah, a Texas real estate broker, to renew her license she must:

a) complete 10 hours of continuing education

b) complete 15 hours of continuing education

c) complete 20 hours of continuing education

d) retake the real estate exam

62. The most probable price that an informed purchaser might pay is the:

a) sales price

b) broker price opinion

c) market value

d) assessed value

63. A lender prequalifies a couple for a loan amount up to $375,000 with a 3.5% down payment. What booklet must he give them within three days of application?

a) an information booklet prepared by HUD

b) a booklet on the explanation of closing costs

c) Regulation – Z booklet

c) HUD-1 booklet

64. When a borrower makes a down payment of less than 20% and gets an FHA loan, what monthly charge should they expect to be added to their mortgage payment?

a) property taxes

b) funding fee

c) mortgage insurance premium

d) equity loan payment

65._____ backs rural development loans.

a) a life insurance company

b) FHA

c) Freddie Mac

d) Ginnie Mae

66. The sales comparison approach is also known as the:

a) appraisal process

b) market data

c) replacement cost

d) cost

67. What are the specific violations in the Texas Deceptive Trade-Practices Act (DPTA) called?

a) obsolescence

b) deceptive trade practices

c) laundry list

d) non-conformities

68. A buyer purchasing a previously occupied single-family residence does not receive written notice of a property's condition by signing. How long does the buyer have to terminate the contract after notice arrives?

a) 10 days

b) 5 days

c) 7 days

d) 30 days

69. If a three-family home is valued at $769,000 and the cap rate is 9%, what is the annual net operating income?

a) $69,210

b) $85,444

c) $100,000

d) $71,000

70. Tim inherits his family's farm, which has suffered years of neglect. He decides to take an equity loan on the property, so his realtor orders an appraisal. While doing the appraisal, the appraiser sees obvious physical deterioration and notices that a bathroom was never added to the home; it still has an outhouse. The lack of an indoor bathroom is a _____.

a) functional obsolescence

b) physical deterioration

c) economic obsolescence

d) accrued depreciation

71. Another name for the Federal Fair Housing Act is:
_____.

a) Fair housing

b) Title VIII of the Civil Rights Act of 1968

c) Federal Civil Rights Act of 1966

d) Consumer Protection Law

72. What is the process that occurs when the state determines the distribution of intestate property?

a) escheat

b) writ of possession

c) transfer of real property

d) title by descent

73. All of these are grounds for license suspension or revocation EXCEPT:

a) commingling personal and business funds

b) acting as an undisclosed dual agent

c) owing no fiduciary duties to clients while acting as a facilitator

d) practicing real estate with an inactive license

74. All have right of survivorship EXCEPT:

a) tenancy in common

b) tenancy by entirety

c) joint tenancy

d) none of the above

75. The best form of ownership is:

a) *pur autre vie*

b) leasehold

c) fee simple

d) freehold

76. Mary and John owned their home as joint tenants until Mary died. Which statement is true?

a) John now has to sell his home.

b) If there is a loan on the property, the lender will call the loan due.

c) John has become the sole owner.

d) John will have to move.

77. How many members of the Texas Real Estate Commission (TREC) have to represent the general public?

a) 3

b) 6

c) 9

d) 13

78. A licensed agent who is associated with a brokerage is a:

a) broker

b) salesperson

c) processor

d) escrow agent

79. Overlooked by many homeowners, which is NOT a cost of owning a home?

a) repairs

b) interest paid on the mortgage loan

c) personal property taxes

d) maintenance

80. Which is MOST likely to influence a person's decision to purchase a home in a certain location?

a) street signage

b) school ratings

c) high number of planned unit developments

d) loan types

81. A single TRELA violation can lead to which type of damages?

a) none

b) treble

c) escheat

d) loss of sponsorship

82. Which of the following does not have to be in writing to be binding?

a) offers

b) acceptance

c) deeds

d) none of the above

83. Mr. and Mrs. Sellers signed the purchase and sales agreement in which they are selling their home to the Buyer family. Although the Buyers have moved forward in getting all inspections, appraisals, etc., ordered on the property, the Sellers are now feeling sad and they desire to terminate the contract. Which statement is true?

a) they are the owners and maintain the right to terminate the contract at any time

b) they may be forced to sell their home as the contract is legal and binding

c) if they offer to return the Buyers' deposit and pay other incurred expenses, the Buyers must accept this and allow them to terminate the contract

d) none of the above

84. Which of the following ads will require more disclosures?

a) We have no money down loans.

b) VA, FHA and conventional loans offered here

c) APR is 4.5% on a 30-year fixed loan

d) The interest rate is 4.375% per year

85. A missing _____ could cause a home not to pass an FHA inspection.

a) refrigerator

b) freestanding stove

c) cooktop

d) washer/dryer

86. Larry is purchasing a home that has $20,000 in needed repairs but he doesn't have $20,000. What loan is a good option for him?

a) FHA 203(b)

b) FHA 203(k)

c) FHA 203(c)

d) FHA

87. The minimum age in Texas to receive a salesperson's license is:

a) 21

b) 25

c) 16

d) 18

88. In Texas, when a broker works with an out-of-state broker who is not licensed in Texas, what may occur?

a) splitting fee

b) equity share

c) co-broker

d) commission split

89. In Texas, a salesperson is _____ by a broker.

a) represented

b) co-broker

c) sponsored

d) none of the above

90. A Texas law that protects consumers is:

a) TREC

b) TRELA

c) Consumer credit laws

d) Deceptive Trade Practices Act

91. Jim does a lot of home improvement projects, and he built a shed on his neighbor Jerry's land. Jim has used this shed continuously for over 20 years. Jim can pursue a claim of _____ in order to gain title to the property.

a) adverse possession

b) eminent domain

c) servient tenement

d) concurrent ownership

92. An ad reads "two-story traditional 1,500-square-foot home in Houston, Texas for sale. Asking $223,000. Please call Rhonda at 830-455-8234." From a legal perspective, the ad is missing:

a) Rhonda's last name

b) Rhonda disclosing that she is a broker

c) number of bedrooms and bathrooms

d) Rhonda disclosing her brokerage's name and that she is a licensed broker

93. What is a broker's commission fee percent if she sells a building for $673,225 and her earned fee is $16,830.62?

a) 2.5%

b) 6.5%

c) 3.5 %

d) 4.0%

94. Another name for some loan fees is:

a) application fee

b) credit report fee

c) discount points

d) broker's fees

95. The Federal Civil Rights Act was passed in:

a) 1968

b) 1866

c) 1868

d) 1986

96. The _____ sets the minimum requirements for appraisals.

a) RESPA

b) MLS

c) TILA

d) USPAP

97. A section is:

a) 2 square miles

b) a city block

c) 27,878,400 square feet

d) 43,560 acres

98. Which act governs plumbers and electricians in inspection and appraisal?

a) HUD

b) Texas Structural Pest Control Act

c) DTPA

d) SFR

99. Which is not covered under the fair housing laws?

a) a SFR that is corporate-owned

b) elderly housing that meets certain Department of Housing and Urban Development guidelines

c) a two-to-four-unit dwelling that is not owner-occupied

d) a home owned by an individual who owns more than three properties

100. Within a three-year period, an owner has been found guilty of sending discriminatory letters to his tenants. The owner may have to pay civil penalties up to _____ if this is his first offense:

a) $25,000

b) $10,000

c) $50,000

d) $20,000

Real Estate Sales Exam I Answers

1. b. The couple (owner) is conveying title to the real property.

2. a. 1 acre = 43,560 square feet   43,560 * .25 = 10,890 square feet

3. d. None of the above. The property was a principal residence which was lived in two of the past five years with a profit less than $500,000.

4. d. The effective gross amount is $4,500 + $150 (the sum of all income generated).

5. a. The transaction is "non-arms length" because they are related.

6. c. The children are generally protected under Chapter 151B (Fair Housing) except when an occupant requests a temporary lease

7. b. Sub-agency requires that the listing broker obtain written permission from the seller and that the fiduciary duties are to the seller.

8. a. To eliminate the mortgage insurance premium, the loan-to-value must be below 80%.

9. a. A contract is defined as an agreement between two or more persons or entities and can be written or oral.

10. a. This is not an arm's length transaction, because the brother and sister are related; therefore, the sold price cannot be included with arm's length sales comps.

11. c. Emblements are crops that are annually cultivated.

12. b. Each spouse has equal interest in property acquired during marriage.

13. c. Because the borrower has transferred the property, the lender is allowed to demand full payment.

14. c. The broker must deposit escrow funds in the appropriate title, trust, or escrow account. The money must be deposited by the end of the second business day.

15. d. Fannie Mae and Freddie Mac purchase conventional loans.

16. b. Processors prepare the loan package for the underwriter.

17. b. Mortgage brokers bring borrowers together with lenders.

18. a. The first step to obtaining home loan financing is to submit the application.

19. c. VA loans offer 100% financing and include a funding fee.

20. b. Shared equity is when the lender offers a low interest rate in exchange for a portion of the equity.

21. c. This contract was written with a financing contingency in which the purchaser was given a date by which to secure financing.

22. a. The property manager is required to make and keep a copy of collected funds for three years.

23. d. Under the Lead Paint Law, the buyer gets 10 days to test for evidence of lead paint.

24. c. 6 of the members of the TREC must be licensed brokers.

25. b. The cost approach is used when the appraiser has difficulty finding comps.

26. a. FNMA purchases conventional loans.

27. a. The new mortgage will include the remaining balance on the existing first mortgage.

28. d. The lender must do an appraisal, ensure the borrower has means to repay the mortgage and can meet the lender's credit score.

29. b. Points charged by a lender are to lower the rate for the buyer.

30. d. RESPA prohibits several types of payments to persons who did not perform a service.

31. a. The term is for six years.

32. c. The Civil Rights Act of 1966 prohibits discrimination on the basis of race in the sale, lease, or other transfer of real or personal property.

33. b. A HUD-1 is also known as a Uniform Settlement Statement.

34. a. The title insurance companies protect the holder from defects in the title.

35. c. An exclusive right to sell listing allows the broker to receive a commission no matter who sells the property.

36. d. Eminent domain gives the government the right to take private property for public use.

37. c. In net lease, the tenant pays the maintenance and operating expenses.

38. a. Because he made energy-efficient improvements he has weatherized his home.

39. b. Find the answer by taking the cost of the home $319,750 and multiplying it by 20% or .20.

40. c. Subtract the listing broker's commission percentage from the total commission percentage. Then multiply that result by the home sales price. Then multiply that number by the listing broker's split with his agent.   6% - 3.5% = 2.5% x $449,000 = $11,225 x 55% = $6,174.

41. b. The lender only offered one loan type to homebuyers purchasing in the area which is more than likely a low-to-moderate income area.

42. d. To be a broker in Texas, you must have two-years experience as a licensed salesperson.

43. c. Licensees in Texas must be at least 18.

44. a. FHA insured loans protect the lender in the event the borrower defaults.

45. c. Homesteads are protected from most creditors under Texas law. The other liens may be used.

46. d. Non-freehold estates give the holder of the estate the right to occupy the property until the end of the lease.

47. a. Notice to vacate is placed outside a residence when a lessee is not adhering to the terms of the lease.

48. a. Short sale is when the bank gives the homeowner the permission to sell his home when he owes more than it is worth.

49. d. "OLD CAR" is an acronym used to remember agents' fiduciary duties to their clients.

50. c. Divide the profit (commission) Mrs. Ramirez made off the sell by the house sale price. $19,500/$325,000 = .06

51. d. A broker cannot mix business and personal funds, refuse to pay clients their escrow funds when requested, or violate TRELA.

52. c. When no heirs can be found, the state can lay claim to the property.

53. a. Joint tenants can transfer title but the new owner becomes a tenant in common with the other joint tenants. For joint tenancy to be valid everyone must go on title at the same time.

54. d. A purchase money mortgage is when the seller holds the financing for the borrower.

55. b. Price/square foot is found by dividing the price by the square feet. 328,000/2,980 = 110.

56. d. Multiply the lot dimensions 378 x 296 = 111,888 square feet. An acre is 43,560 square feet; therefore, divide the area and multiply the result by 43,560. $198,000/111,888 X 43,560 = $77,042.

57. c. New landlord leases property back to the tenant.

58. a. Divide the down payment by the sales price. $104,250/$417,000 = .25 or 25%.

59. a. Licensees must comply with subpoenas from the TREC. The matter may be referred to the district court.

60. c. In a balloon mortgage the final lump sum is due at the balloon termination date.

61. b. A broker or sales agent must take 15 hours of continuing education classes to renew his or her license.

62. c. Market value is the most probable price that an informed buyer will pay.

63. a. Per RESPA, a lender or mortgage broker must give a borrower a copy of a HUD-prepared information booklet within three days of application.

64. c. FHA provides mortgage insurance to protect the lender in case of default; the borrower pays a monthly fee along with their mortgage payment.

65. d. The Government National Mortgage Association (Ginnie Mae) is a major purchaser of government-backed mortgage loans.

66. b. The market data approach is also known as the comparison approach.

67. c. The Texas Deceptive Trade-Practices Act (DPTA) established a list of specific violations called a laundry list.

68. b. In Texas, a seller must provide written notice of property conditions before signing. A buyer has 7 days to void the contract after receiving notice if it is not provided before signing.

69. a. value x cap rate = net operating Income

    769,000 x .09 = 69,210

70. a. Functional obsolescence highlights various features that are no longer considered desirable.

71. b. The Federal Fair Housing Act broadened the prohibitions against discrimination in housing to include sex, race, color, religion, national origin, familial status, and handicap in connection with the sale or rental of housing or vacant land.

72. d. The process of the state dividing intestate property is title by descent or intestate succession.

73. c. A facilitator (non-agent) owes no fiduciary duties to clients

74. a. Tenancy in common does not have right of survivorship. Tenancy by entirety is a form of joint tenancy and they both have right of survivorship.

75. c. Fee simple is a type of freehold estate and is the best form of ownership because the owner has the right to occupy or rent the property, sell or transfer ownership, build on and mine for minerals and restrict or allow the use of the property to others.

76. c. Joint tenancy includes the right of survivorship; the surviving co-owners share equally in the deceased owner's interest.

77. a. There are nine members of the TREC. Three are members of the general public.

78. b. A licensed agent who is associated with a brokerage is a salesperson.

79. c. Personal property taxes are taxes on personal property, not real property.

80. b. School ratings can influence whether a person purchases in a certain area.

81. b. In Texas, a single violation is given equal weight as a series of violations. The individual may be obliged to pay treble damages (three times the original amount).

82. a. Contracts must be written to be legally binding.

83. b. Because the contract is legal and binding, if the Sellers don't move forward, they will be in breach of contract and the Buyers can sue for specific performance.

84. a. The ad should disclose the loan amount, down payment, APR, and terms of repayment.

85. c. FHA minimum property guidelines state that the home must be delivered in safe, secure and sound condition. A freestanding stove could be considered personal property, but a cooktop (because it is attached) is a part of the home.

86. b. FHA 203(k) is FHA's Rehabilitation Loan Insurance Program.

87. d. Texas's minimum age for a real estate license is 18.

88. a. Fees and commissions may not be split with unlicensed individuals. It is possible, however, to share fees with a broker licensed in another state who is not licensed in Texas.

89. c. The agent is sponsored by a broker. Loss of sponsorship could result in a loss of license.

90. d. The Deceptive Trade Practices Act was created to protect consumers from unscrupulous business practices.

91. a. Adverse possession is a method of acquiring title to another person's property through court action after continuous use for more than 20 years.

92. d. The broker must disclose her name and that she is a licensed broker.

93. a. Divide the total commission earned by the sales price. $16,830.62/$673,225 = .025 x 100 = 2.5%.

94. c. Discount points are loan fees that the buyer can pay to get a lower interest rate.

95. b. The Federal Civil Rights Act was passed in 1866 to prohibit discrimination on the basis of race.

96. d. The Uniform Standards of Professional Appraisal Practice (USPAP) sets the minimum requirement for appraisals.

97. c. A section is 640 acres. (640 acres/acre) x 43,560 square feet = 27,878,400 square feet.

98. b. The Texas Structure Pest Control Act is used to determine if plumbers, electricians, carpenters, and structural and pest control are in compliance.

99. b. The Federal Fair Housing Act does not cover housing for the elderly that meets certain HUD guidelines.

100. b. Under the Federal Fair Housing Act, a person can be found liable for civil penalties up to $10,000 for the first offense.

Real Estate Sales Exam II

1. MY TOWN Realty gets a listing to sell a home. The broker appoints one of his sales agents (with permission of the sellers), Melissa to represent the sellers. During one of the open houses, a couple comes in and decides to make an offer, so they call the broker at MY TOWN, who then assigns one of his other sales agents, Keith to represent the buyers. In this case the broker is acting as a:

a) non-agent

b) designated seller's and buyer's agent/dual agent

c) single agent

d) principal agent

2. A buyer secures a first mortgage for $243,750, puts down 15%, and the seller carries back 10%. What was the sales price of the home if she paid full asking?

a) $250,000

b) $300,000

c) $375,000

d) $325,000

3. All are true statements regarding appraisal reports EXCEPT?

a) they can be orally delivered

b) they must be delivered on the Uniform Residential Appraisal Report

c) must use guidelines set forth by USPAP

d) they can be delivered in writing

4. Seller competition in the market usually results in:

a) higher home prices

b) lower home prices

c) anticipation

d) progression

5. The disposition, control, right of possession, and enjoyment are all:

a) zoning ordinances

b) intangibles

c) corporeal

d) the bundle of rights of ownership

6. All are real property EXCEPT:

a) air rights

b) refrigerator

c) oak tree

d) pond

7. Mr. Sanders and his family bought a property 10 years ago. It has increased in value by 2% every year that he has owned it. If he bought it for $450,000, what is it worth now?

a. $540,000

b. $465,000

c. $501,000

d. $525,000

8. A church, which has 501(c)3 status is exempt from paying:

a) a mortgage

b) Income taxes

c) hazard insurance

d) licensing fees

9. A lender will typically not allow front ratio to exceed which of the following?

a) 28%

b) 30%

c) 17%

d) 32%

10. Matthew has a job offer in another city, and he decides to sublet his apartment until the lease runs out. What must he do?

a) call a lawyer

b) contact a broker

c) get landlord approval

d) create an ad

11. Even though Jennifer's lease ended over a month ago, she has not moved out. What type of tenancy does she now have?

a) tenancy at will

b) tenancy for years

c) tenancy for period to period

d) tenancy at sufferance

12. Realtors are members of the:

a) NAREB

b) NRA

c) NAR

d) REBAC

13. A lender needs to set a listing price on one of their foreclosed homes. They will more than likely order a(n):

a) mortgage payment history

b) appraisal

c) assessed value report

d) BPO

14. Which one is an example of commercial real estate?

a) a 21-unit apartment complex

b) a store for rent

c) a storefront with apartments on the second floor

d) loft apartments

15. Which lien would take precedence?

a) priority lien

b) judgment lien

c) mechanic's lien

d) tax lien

16. Emblements refers to:

a) real property

b) *fructus naturales*

c) natural fruit

d) annually cultivated crops

17. An exploration company purchases the rights to any minerals and oil from an owner. The owner now owns all rights EXCEPT the following:

a) subsurface

b) water

c) air

d) surface

18. In Texas, what words must be included in the deed to grant ownership?

a) gift deed

b) grant note

c) words of conveyance

d) purchase of intent

19. Cheri was so happy when she received checks from her lender that she could use to pay her contractor. She took out a(n)_____mortgage.

a) equity

b) land sales

c) purchase money mortgage

d) primary

20. Bill negotiated the lease for his new apartment on the phone and told the landlord that he could sign the lease and meet in person within three days. However, Bill experienced an emergency and had to fly out of town right away, so he told his twin brother Larry to meet the landlord and sign the lease for him. The lease is:

a) valid

b) void

c) voidable

d) illegal

21. In two days, Jackie was anticipating going to her home loan closing, but instead she received a call from her agent that the home had an old second lien on it that the seller said he had paid off. What term best describes the title?

a) the title is free and clear

b) the title is encumbered

c) the title is vested

d) the title is clouded

22. Due to the economy and a loss of jobs in the area, home prices have fallen by 46% and are now valued at about $372,000. Based on the information, what was the average home price before the values fell?

a) $866,000

b) $689,000

c) $668,000

d) $888,888

23. A landlord in Texas has a notice to vacate for a tenant, but the tenant has a large dog inside the residence. What should the landlord do?

a) place the notice on the exterior of the main entrance

b) phone the tenant

c) call animal control

d) wait for the tenant

24. A couple, who had their home listed with Any Town Brokerage, hosted a Christmas party. One of the guests from the party loved the home and came back over to ask them several questions about the house and to get a formal tour. He ended up purchasing the home and the sellers did not have to pay Any Town Brokerage a commission. What type of listing did they have with Any Town?

a) dual

b) net

c) open

d) exclusive agency

25. An apartment purchaser receives shares and a limited partnership. What type of apartment was purchased?

a) condo

b) cooperative

c) multi-unit

d) three-family unit

26. A broker refuses to show a family a home of interest to them because it is not in the "right neighborhood." What is occurring?

a) blockbusting

b) panic peddling

c) steering

d) less favorable treatment

27. Balance contributes to value when:

a) there is homogeneity in a neighborhood

b) there are diverse land uses

c) there is conformity

d) there is regression

28. If an agent is found to have violated TRELA, how much money may he be fined?

a) $1,000

b) $600

c) $800

d) $1,200

29. Mrs. Tenant vacated her apartment because her landlord turned off the water. This was a(n):

a) adverse eviction

b) lease back

c) constructive eviction

d) contractual eviction

30. In a 99-year lease, the buyer typically receives all bundle of rights EXCEPT:

a) enjoyment

b) possession

c) control of use

d) none of the above

31. Which law applies only to properties with buildings constructed before 1978?

a) Fair Housing Act

b) Sherman Antitrust Law

c) TRELA

d) Lead-Based Paint Disclosure Law

32. Violet lives in a condominium and defaults on her payments and taxes. How does this affect the other condominium owners?

a) it does not

b) they also default

c) they must increase their payments to compensate

d) they risk losing their properties

33. What type of tenancy occurs when the tenant remains on the property after the lease has expired?

a) tenant at will

b) tenant with written lease

c) tenant at sufferance

d) tenant by regulation

34. Another name for a tenant at will is _____.

a) yearly lease

b) common tenancy

c) sublease

d) month-to-month

35. A former agent with a lapsed license helps her friends find a home. She introduces herself as an agent and does not reveal that her license is expired. As a favor, she reduces her standard commission. What has she violated?

a) nothing

b) competency

c) accounting

d) TRELA

36. Which of the following is a TRELA exemption?

a) salespeople without sponsorship

b) owners who act for themselves

c) unlicensed brokers

d) brokers serving as fiduciaries

37. A seller will pay 3% in closing costs. If the sales price is $378,499 and the buyer is putting down a 20% down payment, which is the amount paid by the seller?

a) $2,270

b) $9,084

c) $3,000

d) $11,355

38. In Texas, it is legal for property owners to access what information for property managers?

a) credit history

b) job history

c) license

d) DWI history

39. A salesperson's sponsorship is terminated by one broker, how long does she have to change sponsorship and notify TREC?

a) 10 days

b) 14 days

c) 60 days

d) 90 days

40. What is NOT a fiduciary duty?

a) disclosure

b) accounting

c) faithful performance

d) loyalty

41. If you are a tenant in a property that has been sold, your tenancy will:

a) terminate and you must immediately move out

b) automatically convert to a written lease with the lender

c) automatically turn into a tenancy at will

d) turn into an option to purchase

42. Sharon was told that her front and back end numbers were 48/55 and that she did not qualify for a home loan at this time. These are called _____.

a) LTV

b) qualifying ratios

c) cost per unit

d) income to debt ratios

43. Farmer Jedd has _____ rights in that he is able to allow his horses to drink from the river next to his property.

a) mineral

b) air and surface

c) littoral

d) riparian

44. A broker alters a deed of trust. What is the broker doing?

a) practicing law

b) performing fiduciary duties

c) faithful performance

d) accounting

45. An escrow account must be maintained by_____.

a) brokers

b) salespeople

c) licensees

d) fiduciary

46. Mitzi is a licensed agent but no longer wishes to perform real estate. The only thing she needs to do is:

a) send a resignation letter to her broker

b) send a resignation letter to the commission

c) not pay the renewal fee

d) tell the Board members in person

47. In Texas, a first time homebuyer is someone who hasn't owned a property for _____ years.

a) 4

b) 5

c) never owned a home

d) 3

48. The Taxpayer Relief Act was passed in:

a) 1997

b) 1986

c) 1977

d) 2001

49. Flood insurance is:

a) always optional

b) required in certain areas

c) automatically included in the hazard insurance policy

d) only available to homeowners purchasing properties financed by rural housing

50. Patty has gotten a loan pre-approval from Conservative Trust Bank. More than likely, her housing expense ratio does not exceed _____ percent.

a) 38

b) 20

c) 28

d) 33

51. **How long must disclosures be kept in Texas?**

a) 1 year

b) 6 years

c) 3 years

d) 8 years

52. **Under the cost approach, the formula for determining value is:**

a) Replacement or Reproduction Cost – Accrued Depreciation + Land Value = Value

b) Accrued Depreciation – Replacement or Reproduction Cost + Land Value = Value

c) Replacement or Reproduction Cost + Accrued Depreciation - Land Value = Value

d) Replacement or Reproduction Cost + Land Value – Accrued Depreciation = Value

53. **These are in a protected class:**

a) children

b) veterans

c) elderly

d) all of the above

54. **A broker told an elderly couple that for $3,000 she could help them get their loan modified to a more affordable payment, but after the couple gave her the money she disappeared. What law has the broker violated?**

a) The Federal Civil Rights Act

b) The Texas Property Code

c) Texas Lead Paint Law

d) DTPA

55. The _____ pledges the property as collateral.

a) mortgage lien

b) mortgage deed

c) mortgage note

d) collateralization note

56. Land, "bundle of legal rights," and permanent, additions made by humans are:

a) personal property

b) emblements

c) real property

d) real estate

57. Lisa and Mike are remodeling their home. The contractor unloads a truckload of drywall and tile in front of their house. The delivered items are:

a) personal property

b) encumbrances

c) real property

d) real estate

58. Which is NOT one of the "bundle of rights"?

a) right to transfer the home to a relative

b) right to live in the home

c) right to refuse entry into the home

d) right to run a neighborhood casino

59. Which economic characteristic of real estate is best represented by the following example? Two identical homes built by the same developer are located on Milford Street, which is a street that separates two cities, Old City and New City. House A is in New City and sits on the west side of the street and House B sits on the east side of the street and is in Old

City. Because it is a newer area, homeowners believe that the school district in New City is better than Old City.

a) relative scarcity

b) area preference

c) supply and demand

d) improvements

60. A granddaughter inherited a home worth about $225,000 that her grandparents had lived in for 50 years. This home had a great deal of sentimental value to her and because of that she decided to remodel the home to her taste, which cost her well over $380,000 in remodeling costs. While the home's value increased to $300,000, the appraiser did tell her that she over-improved the home for that neighborhood. What type of value does this home now have?

a) objective

b) indestructible

c) subjective

d) immobility

61. In Texas, which of the following is meant to prevent and reduce fraud?

a) The Texas Property Code

b) The Fair Housing Act

c) DTPA

d) The Statute of Frauds

62. If you bought your home 20 years ago for $80,000 and now the value is $225,000, at what percent did the house appreciate each year?

a. 23%

b. 7%

c. 12%

d. 9%

63. Who can issue a junior mortgage?

a) Freddie Mac

b) the VA

c) the seller

d) RHS

64. Kelley, Marvin and Andrea are joint tenants. When Andrea dies, Kelley and Marvin remain as joint tenants. When Marvin dies, Kelley now holds title as a sole owner. Kelley now holds title in _____.

a) common

b) severalty

c) entirety

d) life estate

65. Greg has an oceanfront property where he is able to enjoy the ocean at any time. He has _____ rights.

a) bundle of rights

b) alluvial

c) riparian

d) littoral

66. A(n) _____ is divided into 36 sections.

a) city

b) township

c) borough

d) acre

67. In a deed, *et ux* means:

a) and wife

b) everyone

c) and others

d) and husband

68. Abraham bought a property and later learned that his great grandfather's father may have owned that property. What can he order that will show the property ownership history?

a) deed of trust

b) legal description

c) certificate of title

d) chain of title

69. A chattel mortgage would more than likely be used in a transaction with all of the following EXCEPT:

a) car

b) furniture

c) single family residence

d) mobile home

70. A developer plans to build a new subdivision that is pedestrian-friendly. The homes will be on small lots, but the community will have several "green" areas with parks and common areas for the residents. This type of design is known as _____.

a) communal property

b) clustering

c) commingling

d) canvassing

71. Mrs. James' husband passed away about six months ago and because she is on fixed income she is finding it difficult to meet all of her expenses due to her husband's remaining

medical bills. Because she owns her home free and clear and she would like to remain in it, what loan product might be an option for her?

a) junior mortgage

b) HELOC

c) primary mortgage

d) HECM

72. Which is NOT a method used to satisfy the requirement for legal description in a deed?

a) the Torrens System

b) the metes and bounds system

c) the lot and block system

d) the government survey system

73. Juliet has lived in her apartment for four months and loves it. Because summer is approaching and she does not have air conditioning, she's decided to replace her dining room lighting fixture with a ceiling fan. The ceiling fan will now be a(n):

a) riparian right

b) easement

c) real property

d) personal property

74. A hardship associated with acquiring rental property is:

a) the law of increasing returns

b) lack of reserves

c) negative amortization

d) redlining

75. A broker's license is NOT required:

a) when an individual sells his candy store business to another individual

b) when he offers to list real property for sale

c) when he offers to sell his parents' home

d) in exchange for one month's rent, negotiate the rental of real estate for another individual

76. The ADA is the:

a) American Disabled Vets Act

b) American Disposition of Realty Act

c) American Disposal Act

d) American with Disabilities Act

77. Misty works as a sales agent under Real Time Realty; she is an independent contractor. She should expect all of the following EXCEPT:

a) to assume responsibility for paying her own income tax

b) to be compensated on production

c) to receive employee benefits from the broker

d) that she and the broker will have a written contract

78. Manny and Lisa purchased their home six years ago for $325,000 when they put down 10%. Their interest rate was 6.5% and after making 72 monthly payments, their loan balance was $268,901.06. Assuming the current market value and the sales price are the same, how much equity does the homeowner have?

a) $32,500

b) $56,098.94

c) $29,200

d) none of the above

79. Every homeowner is entitled to the following income tax deductions EXCEPT:

a) loan interest on second homes

b) property taxes

c) discount points

d) penalty-fee withdrawals up to $10,000 from an IRA

80. Byron, a first-time homebuyer, bought his home for $72,500 with an FHA loan. The contract was executed April 28th, 2010. Because he had a 60-day escrow, he finally got his keys on June 30th, 2010. How much tax credit money should he expect to get back if he has no other tax liabilities?

a) $7,250

b) $500

c) $8,000

d) $7,500

81. Which physical characteristic of real estate best describes the following: two parcels of land are not identical:

a) homogeneity

b) immobility

c) non-homogeneity

d) a physical characteristic of land

82. Which of the following are uses of real property?

a) residential

b) grazing cattle

c) cemetery

d) all of the above

83. The first real estate license law was passed in _____ in 1919.

a) Massachusetts

b) New York

c) California

d) Texas

84. A cookie shop owner needs to move to a larger location. When he removed the oven, he repaired the holes from the bolts on the walls and the floors. The oven was a(n):

a) fixture

b) trade fixture

c) piece of real property

d) appurtenance

85. The section on the 1003 that deals with the race or ethnicity and sex of an applicant is data collected under the:

a) Home Mortgage Disclosure Act

b) Community Redevelopment Act

c) Fair Housing Act

d) Federal Civil Rights Act

86. Broker Connie says the following phrases to her clients: "Better sell the house before too many of them move into the neighborhood." "There goes the neighborhood." These are examples of:

a) redlining

b) steering

c) blockbusting

d) commingling

87. Randy meets with loan officer Jackie so she can prequalify him for a loan. After talking with Randy she learns that he is unmarried and decides to halt the application process. Randy calls her several times only to receive voicemail. Since it appears that Jackie is discriminating against Randy on the basis of marital status, what law is she violating?

a) The Civil Rights Act of 1964

b) The ADA

c) The Federal Fair Housing Act of 1866

d) ECOA

88. Which is NOT a purpose of the License Law?

a) raise revenue

b) protect the public from incompetent brokers

c) prescribe minimum standards for licensing brokers

d) protect licensed brokers and salespersons from unfair or improper competition

89. Which is NOT a public control?

a) police power

b) eminent domain

c) water rights

d) environmental regulations

90. Ms. Mary owned the land adjacent to her church and decided to grant it to the church as long as it is used to build a recreation center for the church's youth. This type of estate is known as:

a) fee simple

b) determinable fee

c) legal fee

d) conventional life estate

91. Sonja gave her $3,500 earnest money deposit to her sales agent. What should her sales agent do next?

a) deposit the check in his (the sales agent's) personal checking account

b) give the check to the office's transaction coordinator who will then put it in the company's escrow account

c) cash the check and give Sonja a receipt

d) give the check to the office's transaction coordinator who will then place the check in a file folder with Sonja's name on it along with the contract, and store them safely in the file cabinet

92. Johnny and Donna visit a new home development and fall in love with the model homes. All of the homes in this subdivision have only one level. After picking a floor plan they like, they ask the sales agent what the cost would be to add a second story media room and bathroom. The sales agent advises the couple that the developers have created a _____ _____ that does not permit two-story homes in the subdivision.

a) planning and zoning law

b) inverse condemnation

c) public control

d) deed restriction

93. Ted received a letter stating that the lender had obtained a deficiency judgment against him. Which scenario best fits what has happened to Ted?

a) One of his creditors from a credit card put his account in collections then filed a judgment against him.

b) The home was sold in an auction for the amount he owed, but because there were no funds to pay the agents, the lenders paid it and are now suing Ted for the deficiency.

c) Ted's loan balance and fees were more than the home sold for at foreclosure sale; therefore the lender will claim Ted's other assets in order to satisfy the indebtedness.

d) none of the above

94. When working on behalf of a seller or buyer, an agent must exhibit good business judgment, trust and honesty. This creates a(n) _____ _____.

a) fiduciary relationship

b) faithful performance

c) implied authority

d) special agent

95. Keith is selling his five-unit complex. He should be prepared to bring all documents below EXCEPT:

a) tax returns

b) lease agreements

c) maintenance contracts

d) estoppels letters from the tenants

96. Baker and Johnson Partnership decides to sell off some their real estate. If each partner holds title as tenants in common, which signatures will be required to convey the real estate?

a) Only one signature is required since it is a partnership.

b) Since each partner holds title, they will each have to sign.

c) They can sign with a stamp in the name of their partnership.

d) Whenever a partnership sells real estate, only two signatures are required no matter how many partners there are.

97. Theron and Perry are neighbors. Theron builds a fence and two feet of it extends into Perry's property. The fence is an example of a(n):

a) eminent domain

b) encumbrance

c) encroachment

d) easement by necessity

98. A couple residing in a community property state has been married for five years. During the marriage, the wife's grandfather decides to give each of his grandchildren their inheritance, which is one of his income producing properties. The property is:

a) community property

b) sole proprietorship

c) part of a land trust

d) separate property

99. Real estate ownership by a corporation is a(n):

a) tenancy in sufferance

b) tenancy in severalty

c) joint tenancy

d) none of the above as corporations can't own real estate

100. Barbara has been pre-approved for a maximum purchase price of $318,000 based on 90% LTV. What will her down payment be?

a) $10,000

b) $6,400

c) $32,000

d) $23,000

Real Estate Sales Exam II Answers

1. b. Designated buyer's and seller's agent is a designated agent who represents their client and owes fiduciary duties to their client and with the client's permission the agent can be designated by another agent. When the appointing agent designates another agent in the office to represent the other party to the transaction, the broker will also be a dual agent.

2. d. First we need to establish that the borrower's down payment and the seller carryback can be added together and treated like it is the borrower's down payment. Second, find the loan-to- value (LTV) which is $100 - 25 = 75\%$ or .75. Since we are given the loan amount and now have the LTV we can solve for the sales price: $\$243,750/.75 = \$325,000$.

3. b. The appraisal may be done on another form.

4. b. When sellers are competing there is a lot of supply in the market which drives home prices down.

5. d. The bundle of rights are the property rights which include the right of possession, control, enjoyment and disposition.

6. b. The refrigerator is not attached to the house. The owner can take this with him/her therefore it is personal property.

7. a. $450,000 X .02 = $9,000 increased value each year. Take increased value and multiply it by the number of years the property has been owned. $9,000 X 10 = $90,000. Add the total increased value to sales price. $450,000 + $90,000 = $540,000

8. b. Nonprofits are exempt from federal income taxes.

9. a. When lenders use front ratio, they typically will not lend over 28% to anyone.

10. c. In Texas, the landlord must approve a sublet.

11. a. Tenancy at will is a lease without a termination date

12. c. National Association of Realtors

13. d. BPO or broker price opinion is when the mortgage holder gets a broker's opinion of value based on a competitive market analysis.

14. b. Apartments are not considered commercial property.

15. d. Tax liens are given priority over other liens.

16. d. Emblements are cultivated crops.

17. a. Subsurface rights are rights below the earth's surface.

18. c. Deeds must include a granting clause or words of conveyance to be valid that say, "I grant/convey."

19. a. Equity mortgage is when the homeowner takes out a portion of the equity on his property; often lenders will send the borrower checks.

20. c. A voidable contract binds one party but not the other.

21. d. Clouded title is when there is a document, claim, or unreleased lien that may impair the title to real property or make the title doubtful.

22. b. First we need to find the LTV which is 100 - 46 = 54% or .54. $372,000/.54 = $688,889.

23. a. In Texas, the landlord may place the notice to vacate on the exterior if he cannot enter the dwelling.

24. d. An exclusive agency listing means that only one listing broker represents the seller. If the property sells through the efforts of the broker, however, the seller retains the right to sell the property on his own without paying a commission.

25. b. Cooperatives are apartments owned by a corporation that holds titles to the entire cooperative property.

26. c. Steering is directing clients away from certain properties. It violates the Fair Housing Act.

27. b. Balance is when a neighborhood or town has several types of land uses.

28. a. A violation of TRELA may result in a $1,000 fine.

29. c. Constructive eviction is when a landlord has rendered a property uninhabitable and the tenant moves out.

30. b. In a 99-year lease the buyer does not have full ownership.

31. d. The Lead-Based Paint Disclosure Law is meant to protect the public from exposure to lead based paint. It applies to buildings built before 1978.

32. a. Condominiums are separate from each other. Unlike cooperatives, one default does not affect the neighbors.

33. c. Tenancy at sufferance occurs when the tenant remains on the property after the lease expires.

34. d. Month-to-month tenancy is an example of tenancy at will.

35. d. Only licensed agents may perform agent duties. She violated TRELA by representing herself as an agent and by taking the commission.

36. b. Owners who represent themselves do not need to be licensed. They are exempt from TRELA.

37. d. Closing cost can be found by multiplying the sales price by the closing cost percent. $378,499 x .03 = $11,355.

38. d. In Texas, property owners are allowed to check the DWI history of anyone who will need to drive as part of his or her duties.

39. b. Sponsorship is required for salespeople to remain active. If sponsorship is lost, the agent has 10 days.

40. a. Disclosure is not a fiduciary duty. The other answers are.

41. c. Turn into a tenancy at will with the new owner

42. b. Qualifying ratios are calculations to determine whether a borrower can qualify for a mortgage.

43. d. Riparian rights are the rights of a landowner whose property is adjacent to a flowing waterway to use the water.

44. a. Altering contracts is considered practicing law. Brokers are not allowed to practice law.

45. a. Brokers are the only ones allowed to maintain escrow accounts. Salespeople may not maintain the accounts.

46. c. The Board will make her license inactive if she doesn't pay the renewal fee.

47. d. First-time homebuyers in most states are individuals who have not owned a home in the last two to three years.

48. a. The Taxpayer Relief Act was enacted August 5, 1997.

49. b. Flood insurance may be required if any part of the property is in a flood zone.

50. c. The housing ratio is the front end or housing expense and the back end ratio is the total debt ratio; conservative lenders tend to use more conservative ratios.

51. c. Under Texas law, disclosures must be kept for three years.

52. a. The formula for determining value:

Replacement or reproduction cost – accrued depreciation + land value = value

53. d. A protected class is any group of people designated by HUD.

54. d. The DTPA prohibits unfair and deceptive trade practices.

55. b. The mortgage deed pledges the property as collateral.

56. c. Real property is real estate plus bundle of legal rights.

57. a. Personal property is moveable.

58. d. Illegal purpose uses are not included in the "bundle of rights."

59. b. The economic characteristics of real estate are relative scarcity, improvements, permanence of investment, and area preference.

60. c. Subjective value is affected by the relative worth an individual places on a specific item.

61. c. The Statute of Frauds requires certain contracts to be written and signed.

62. d. Take $225,000 - $80,000 = $145,000 to get the increased value. Then take increased value/ purchased price. $145,000/$80,000 =1.8. You can find the annual appreciation rate by 1.8/20 years = 9%.

63. c. The seller can offer to carry back a second mortgage.

64. b. Estate in severalty is sole ownership.

65. d. When a landowner's property borders a large non-flowing body of water such as an ocean, the landowner has the right to enjoy the water.

66. b. A township is divided into 36 sections.

67. a. Abbreviation for the Latin term *et uxor*, meaning wife

68. d. A chain of title is a recorded history of conveyances on a particular property.

69. c. A chattel mortgage is used with personal or moveable property.

70. b. Clustering is when a developer groups home sites on smaller lots and leaves the remaining land for use as common areas.

71. d. A home equity conversion mortgage is another name for a reverse mortgage. This type of mortgage allows an elderly person to remain in their home in which the equity is converted to cash for the homeowner.

72. a. The Torrens System is a system of registering title to land with a public authority.

73. c. The ceiling fan became real property once it got attached to the ceiling.

74. b. Most lenders require three to six months of reserves of the PITI payment when purchasing income property: this often creates a barrier to entry.

75. a. A license is not required when an individual sells his business.

76. d. American with Disabilities Act.

77. c. A broker cannot offer benefits to his/her independent contractors.

78. b. $325,000 - $268,901.06 = $56,098.94

79. d. Only first-time homebuyers can withdraw penalty-free up to $10,000 from their IRA.

80. a. The tax credit was worth 10% of the purchase price.

81. c. No two pieces of land are ever exactly alike.

82. d. All are uses of real property.

83. c. California

84. b. The oven was a trade fixture and because he returned the walls and the floors to their original condition it can be considered personal property.

85. a. The Home Mortgage Disclosure Act (HMDA) requires mortgage lenders to collect and report data to assist in identifying possible discriminatory lending practices.

86. c. Blockbusting is the illegal act of convincing homeowners to sell their properties by suggesting that a protected class is moving into the neighborhood.

87. d. The Equal Credit Opportunity Act prohibits lenders from discriminating against credit applicants on the basis of race, color, religion, national origin, sex, marital status, age or dependence on public assistance.

88. a. The License Law was not enacted to raise revenue.

89. c. Water rights do not fall under public control. The other answers do.

90. b. This is a determinable fee estate in which the estate will come to an end immediately if the specified purpose ceases.

91. b. All earnest money deposits must be held in the company's escrow account.

92. d. Deed restrictions can control from what can be parked in a driveway to the exterior color of the homes.

93. c. When the proceeds of the foreclosure sale do not cover what is owed, the lender may claim other assets to cure the indebtedness.

94. a. A fiduciary relationship requires that an agent exhibit trust, honesty and good business judgment when working on behalf of the principal.

95. a. He does not have to supply his tax returns.

96. b. Each partner will have to sign since they each hold title.

97. c. The fence is an encroachment because it invades the neighbor's land.

98. d. Once the grandfather conveys the property to her it is separate property.

99. b. Because a corporation is a legal entity, corporate real estate ownership is held as tenancy in severalty.

100. c. The down payment is 100 – 90 = 10%. 10% of $318,000 = $31,800 or $32,000.

Real Estate Sales Exam III

1. What indicates the cost of a property while factoring in depreciation, for tax purposes?

a) book value

b) insurance value

c) assessed value

d) loan value

2. A salesperson is renewing a license after the first year. How many classroom review hours must be taken?

a) none

b) 30

c) 15

d) 60

3. An inactive salesperson must do what as part of reactivating licensure?

a) perform acts of brokerage

b) take exam

c) pay renewal fees

d) give notice

4. According to RESPA, what is the maximum amount of property taxes and insurance that a lender can keep in a reserve account?

a) 3 months

b) 2 months

c) 1 month

d) none

5. Arthur, the owner of three two-family homes, decides to enlist the help of a property management company to aid him in managing the properties. What type of contract will he have with the property manager?

a) a multiple listing agreement

b) a rental agreement

c) a management agreement

d) a multiple use agreement

6. The Federal Reserve Board's Regulation B implements_____.

a) Equal Credit Opportunity Act

b) Truth in Lending

c) RESPA

d) Home Mortgage Disclosure Act

7. The Hemsley family bought a vacation home in South Padre Island. Their down payment was 40% and they financed the rest. They became the:

a) mortgagee

b) borrower

c) mortgagor

d) lienor

8. Karen, who purchased her apartment in Dallas for $598,000, tells her friend Samantha that her property tax payment is included in her monthly maintenance fee. Samantha should know that Karen more than likely purchased a:

a) leasehold

b) PUD

c) condo

d) coop

9. The Stemmons family owns 2,000 acres of land with several trees on the property. Every year they sell lumber to a timber company. The cut trees are sold as:

a) real property

b) personal property

c) not considered property since they are not a structure

d) an appurtenance

10. Marla, a vendee, has an equitable interest in the property located at 926 Elm Street, Any Town, Any State 12345. In this case Marla is the:

a) seller

b) grantor

c) purchaser

d) grantee

11. Your home has a fence that was installed around 15 years ago and you have lived there for 12 years. You have continuously used your side of the property for eight years without any problems. Recently your neighbor had his land surveyed and it appears as though your fence is on his land. In Texas, if you continue to use the land and your neighbor doesn't say anything, how many years do you have before you can file for adverse possession?

a) 3

b) 5

c) 8

d) 20

12. An option to purchase a home for $325,000 with 120 days was sold to Heather for $9,000. After 60 days the seller accepted an offer of $305,000 from Heather to purchase the home. Which is true?

a) Heather violated the agreement.

b) Heather loses her option deposit.

c) Both Heather and the seller are in violation of contract law.

d) Heather could make a new offer for $305,000.

13. A property is worth $214,000 and it has $156,000 in liens tied to it. This difference is known as:

a) the assessed value

b) down payment

c) equity

d) leverage

14. Martha and her daughter made an offer on another home based on their current home selling by a certain date. What type of clause was this?

a) financing

b) contingency

c) recession

d) partial performance

15. An agent meets with a client in their home for the first time and the couple decides to sign the listing agreement authorizing the broker as their listing agent. The agent loves the home and believes it would make a great starter home for Jack, her neighbor's son. The agent holds an open house and receives two offers along with Jack's offer. These offers are all very similar. Then just before she (the agent) leaves to present the offers, she gets a new offer which is much better than the current offers. Even though she really wants Jack to get the home, she shows all offers to her client. Which of the six agent responsibilities did the agent demonstrate?

a) loyalty

b) accounting

c) reasonable care

d) confidentiality

16. _____ is when the municipality takes action against a property owner and, through the court land process, attempts to gain ownership of the property.

a) foreclosure

b) eminent domain

c) taking

d) constructive notice

17. Which is true?

a) FHA is hazard insurance

b) FHA guarantees that the borrower will not default on the loan

c) FHA 203(k) loans are for one to four family investment properties only

d) FHA insures the lender against borrower default

18. Which contract is voidable?

a) a painter is contracted to paint a home, but two days before he was to begin the job, the home was destroyed by a hurricane.

b) an owner who grows marijuana in his backyard agrees to sell it to his next door neighbor

c) an older brother who lives with his younger brother because he is mentally challenged and needs supervised care contracts a landscaping company to begin cutting the yard

d) a buyer makes an offer to purchase and includes a financing contingency

19. Frank lives in Austin, Texas, and he received a certified letter that he is in default on his mortgage. How long does he have to reinstate the loan?

a) 30 days

b) 14 days

c) 20 days

d) 60 days

20. Victor's family has a rural homestead. What is the maximum acreage that it can be?

a) 50 acres

b) 200 acres

c) 100 acres

d) 150 acres

21. Another name for the government survey method is _____.

a) the rectangular survey system

b) principal surveys

c) base lines survey method

d) principal meridians

22. Jim and Sally are getting married. What do they need to do to guarantee separate property?

a) agree in writing

b) make separate payments

c) buy things separately

d) nothing

23. What is the penalty for noncompliance of a mechanic's lien law?

a) $1,000 fine

b) $4,000 fine

c) $2,000 fine

d) jail sentence

24. Kiley, a realtor and interior designer is, more than likely a member of these two associations:

a) NRA and AID

b) NAR and ASID

c) NAR and MAR

d) REA and NRA

25. Public employees use a mill to calculate:

a) hazard insurance premiums

b) mortgage interest

c) trash and sewage rates

d) property tax rates

26. Julie owns five acres of land that she wanted to sell to Kelvin for $800,000. But, before she could sell the land to Kelvin, she had to first offer it to Angelica, a holder of the right to purchase the land who decided to exercise her right and follow through with the purchase. What right did Angelica exercise?

a) bundle of rights

b) redemption

c) right of first refusal

d) contingency

27. A developer agrees to purchase 50 acres of land from the owner for $600,000. The owner has agreed to carry back 20%. If the developer takes out a construction loan with a first lien position, the landowner will have to agree to a _____ agreement.

a) subordination

b) percentage lease

c) conformity

d) deferred transfer

28. A listing agreement is a(n):

a) future delivery purchase

b) interest in severalty

c) estimated amount for which a party should exchange hands

d) contract between a broker and seller

29. Depreciation is accounted for in which approach:

a) market value

b) cost

c) comparative market analysis

d) rent history

30. Although Jesse works as an independent contractor under his broker, the broker is still responsible for all of the following EXCEPT:

a) providing a contract which clearly stipulates that Jesse is responsible for paying quarterly federal income tax payments

b) the ethical and legal behavior of Jesse

c) payment of licensing and professional fees

d) provide an agreement which defines compensation amounts

31. What type of insurance protects the buyer from a forgery in the title chain?

a) homeowners' insurance

b) title insurance

c) flood insurance

d) renter's insurance

32. The minimum credit score set by FHA is:

a) 580

b) 530

c) 620

d) FHA has no minimum credit score

33. A hearing panel found that Mary was in violation of the National Association of Realtors Code of Ethics. In addition to receiving a penalty of up to $5,000 what course may she be asked to take?

a) ethics

b) principles of real estate

c) accounting

d) consumer information

34. Which is an example of steering?

a) a lender only offers balloon loans to a certain group of buyers

b) a realtor tells his client to sell his home because one of the neighbors rented his house to a Section 8 tenant

c) an owner decides not to rent his home to a disabled veteran

d) a sales agent begins showing homes to more African Americans in an affluent area because she feels the neighborhood needs to be more integrated

35. Every year Jim and Opal receive an annual allotment of 300 vacation points through their timeshare program. This type of timeshare program is known as:

a) rotation club

b) vacation owner points plan

c) vacation club

d) vacation ownership interest club

36. The following legal description is known as a _____.

Lots 3, 4 and 5 in Block 6 of G. Smith's Subdivision, City of Plano, Collin County, Texas.

a) metes and bounds

b) subdivision plat

c) township squares

d) survey system

37. Margaret receives a letter from her homeowners' association that she needs to replace her roof and garage door. She is very upset because she thought these items were covered by the homeowners' association since her unit is attached to other units. What type of unit does Margaret more than likely own?

a) single family residence

b) cooperative

c) townhome

d) condo

38. What needs to happen for the deed to be acknowledged?

a) signed by both parties

b) signed before a notary

c) transfer of property

d) nothing

39. A real estate broker refers his client to US Home Warranty Company and in return they send the broker a $125 referral fee. This is a violation of:

a) the Comprehensive Environmental Response, Compensation, and Liability Act

b) the Real Estate Settlement Procedures Act

c) Truth in Lending

d) HUD-1

40. What would a seller NOT need to bring when there is a closing on an income-producing property?

a) survey

b) leases

c) estoppel letters

d) operating contract

41. In a condominium development, which would be considered a "limited" common element?

a) pool

b) elevator

c) parking slots assigned to occupants

d) limited access gates

42. Real estate forms are promulgated by _____.

a) TREC

b) TRELA

c) FNMA

d) RESPA

43. One of the most important deadlines in the contract documents is the:

a) home inspection

b) option period

c) loan commitment

d) none of the above

44. A person who feels discriminated against by a realtor should file a written complain should with ____.

a) RESPA

b) TRELA

c) TREC

d) HUD

45. What fits the description of a multifamily dwelling under the Fair Housing Act?

a) five-unit dwelling

b) single unit dwelling

c) four-unit dwelling

d) three-unit dwelling

46. An appraiser will use the _____ approach to estimate the value of a three-family rental home.

a) reproduction

b) income

c) cost

d) sales comparison

47. Jane bought her home for $279,000 and now it's worth $333,000. It has _____ in value.

a) appreciated

b) regressed

c) vested

d) diverged

48. Sally received a letter that her home loan with ABC lending was being transferred to Community Bank. This is known as a(n):

a) takeover

b) assumption

c) assignment

d) aggression

49. When a borrower signs a security agreement where he is promising to pay, he is signing a:

a) deed of trust

b) promissory note

c) bill of sale

d) offer contract

50. A disadvantage of a bridge loan is:

a) the buyer does not have to sell his current home before he purchases his next home

b) the lender might not require the buyer to make monthly payments

c) the buyer can immediately put his home on the market

d) buyers may be prequalified based on two mortgages and they might not meet this requirement

51. Henry's title report suggests that the property he's purchasing is free of legal issues and liens, therefore the property has a(n) _____ title.

a) clear

b) cloudy

c) good

d) efficient

52. In a home loan, which is the collateral?

a) the down payment

b) the equity

c) the property

d) the borrower's liquid assets

53. The date an interest rate is changed is known as the:

a) payment shock

b) balloon maturity date

c) the adjustment date on an adjustable rate loan

d) none of the above

54. Lisa makes an offer on a home and gives her broker a check to let the seller know she is serious. These funds are known as:

a) security deposit

b) earnest money deposit

c) option period deposit

d) down payment

55. Which best describes an easement?

a) When a tenant who is moving out of the storefront he rented takes his cupcake oven

b) A property owner whose land is adjacent to a river swims and fishes in the river

c) A neighbor who accesses his barn by legally crossing part of his neighbor's land

d) The state legally takes back private land to widen the highway

56. A subdivision is:

a) a neighborhood in a community revitalized area

b) a housing development where tracts of land are turned into individual lots

c) when houses in a neighborhood are the same style and color

d) a neighborhood with a homeowners' association board

57. A homebuyer who had limited liquid funds, obtained her home through a nonprofit organization, where she helped build her home with her own labor and services. What type of contribution did she make?

a) sweat equity

b) equity deposit

c) money

d) labor

58. Ben, who recently lost his job, is considering transferring ownership of his home back to his lender as he is having great difficulty making the payments and has been unable to sell it. This is known as:

a) foreclosure

b) deed-in-lieu

c) short sale

d) adverse possession

59. Frances put down $68,000 on a $319,000 property. What percent did Frances put down?

a. 21%

b. 35%

c. 18%

d. 12%

60. According to their lender, a couple must contribute $71,700 in the form of a cashier's check toward the purchase of the $478,000 home they are buying. This amount is known as the:

a) earnest money deposit

b) junior mortgage

c) down payment

d) contingency fee

61. For government loans, which statement is true?

a) They are insured by FHA.

b) They are guaranteed by RHS.

c) They are guaranteed by VA.

d) All of the above.

62. Heather conveyed her interest in a property to her brother, Barry's friend, Mike's parents, Mr. and Mrs. Olsen, the parents of her brother Barry's friend, Mike. Who is the grantee?

a) Mike

b) Mr. and Mrs. Olsen

c) Heather

d) Barry

63. Katy and Mickey's home was completely destroyed during the hurricane storm. When they returned to check the damages, they found their basement completely flooded and everything destroyed as the water level reached up to the second floor. Which insurance will more than likely cover the bulk of the damages?

a) hurricane

b) windstorm

c) flood

d) hazard

64. Which is NOT a liquid asset?

a) money in a savings account

b) 401 K

c) parcel of land

d) stocks

65. A homebuyer used a mortgage broker with Finance World to get her home loan. She used the payment coupon provided to her to mail her first payment to Finance World. Before her second payment was due, she received a letter stating that her loan was being assigned to the Bank of the United States and that the investor Duchess Bank had remained the same. Which is her current lender?

a) Finance World

b) Duchess Bank

c) Bank of the United States

d) Mortgage broker

66. If Justine has power of attorney, what has she been granted?

a) limited or full authority to make decisions on behalf of someone else

b) an opportunity to represent someone in court

c) entrance to law school

d) full power to make medical decisions on behalf of someone else

67. The principal is:

a) that part of the mortgage payment that reduces the remaining balance

b) the remaining balance of the amount borrowed

c) a and b

d) b only

68. Which best describes an encroachment?

a) You legally drive across part of your neighbor's property to access your property.

b) You continuously use your neighbor's driveway for years and he doesn't stop you.

c) You add an illegal second level to your home which completely blocks your neighbor's view to the sea.

d) You allow your horses to drink out of the river which is adjacent to your land.

69. Two sons are joint tenants in a property left to them by their parents. Son A has one child and Son B has four children. In the event Son B passes, who does the property go to?

a) the property is split equally between the five grandchildren

b) the property goes to Son A and his child

c) the property goes to Son B's children

d) the property goes to Son A only

70. Ansley wants to see a visual representation of when her mortgage will be paid off as well as how much money she will be paying in interest each year. This is known as a(n):

a) loan payment schedule

b) amortization schedule

c) interest rate table

d) rate sheet

71. A biweekly payment is one in which:

a) the homeowner will make her mortgage payment every two weeks

b) the homeowner will make her mortgage payment every other month

c) the homeowner will make one payment every month, but on the last month of the year two payments will be made

d) the homeowner will make half of her mortgage payment every two weeks

72. Kelly is told that her ARM loan has an initial interest rate of 5.5% and that as the rate adjusts it can never go above 9%. 9% is the _____ for her loan.

a) buy down

b) APR

c) cap

d) *ad valorem*

73. Texas is a _____ state.

a) community property

b) separate property

c) contingency

d) covenant

74. Henry sells his home to his friend Reese; then Henry gets a letter from his lender demanding full payment. The mortgage included a(n) _____.

a) acceleration clause

b) deed restriction

c) due-on-sale clause

d) covenant of seisin

75. Murray had to go to court to get his property back from his nephew because when he granted him the property he told him that he could not sell alcohol on the premises. What type of estate was this?

a) homestead

b) ordinary with remainder or reversion

c) determinable fee estate

d) fee simple subject to a condition subsequent with right of reentry

76. Which provides the best range of property values on a particular property?

a) competitive market analysis

b) broker price opinions

c) appraisal

d) income approach

77. Jenny and Mike finally found the home of their dreams within their budget of $385,000. They had already been pre-approved for a loan based on 75% loan-to-value. If the sales price is $380,000 but the appraisal came in at $365,500, what is the biggest loan the lender will give them for this home?

a) $288,750

b) $380,000

c) $285,000

d) $274,125

78. Under Truth in Lending (TIL), what would the amount of the down payment be called?

a) commission

b) trigger term

c) down payment

d) licenses fees

79. A broker knows that his clients are willing to pay more than the asking price for a home, but does not divulge this when negotiating an offer. What duty is being practiced?

a) loyalty

b) disclosure

c) confidentiality

d) obedience

80. Willford transfers one of his small rental units to his son for $1.00. What is the transfer tax?

a) $0

b) $1,000

c) $4.45

d) $456

81. Martha pays her taxes and insurance every month inside her mortgage payment. This is known as a _____ mortgage.

a) equity

b) budget

c) escrow

d) negative amortization

82. A very famous couple chooses a city apartment near all of the amenities they enjoy so they don't have to travel out too far and risk being noticed. Their agent notifies them they did not receive approval because the Board believes they will disrupt the peace and quiet currently enjoyed by all the residents. Which best describes this scenario?

a) the condo association can vote in or out whoever they feel is a good match (or not) for the condo development

b) the Board is violating the Civil Rights Act of 1866

c) celebrities are a protected class and must not be discriminated against

d) coops can deny or approve the sale of shares of stock if they feel someone may jeopardize the quiet enjoyment the residents currently enjoy

83. The realtor tells a couple that because of regression, they may have to list their home at a different price than anticipated. Which best describes what is happening?

a) the neighboring homes haven't been updated and modernized as much as the subject property

b) the home has an outdated floor plan

c) the home is in disrepair

d) a school was recently built around the corner

84. When Broker Jamie takes his client's earnest money deposit and puts it in his personal account to tide him over until his next commission check comes, which fiduciary duty is he not living up to?

a) dedication

b) accounting

c) obedience

d) confidentiality

85. A homestead does NOT protect you from which of the following:

a) credit cards

b) the proceeds from the sale of your home

c) a Medicaid lien from a nursing home stay

d) the proceeds from your insurance claim if your home was damaged by fire

86. The following is which type of description commonly used in Texas legal descriptions using distance and direction?

a) reference

b) point of beginning

c) strip

d) metes and bounds

87. Katy has a voluntary lien on her home. Which represents a voluntary lien?

a) mortgage

b) property tax

c) federal IRS

d) mechanic's lien

88. A condominium's rules and regulations are called:

a) canvassing

b) bylaws

c) tenancy

d) amortization

89. A broker is listing a home where he knows a homicide was committed. What is the best course of action?

a) canvassing

b) disclosure

c) maintain confidentiality

d) reduce price

90. Jane has a document, which states she has legal rights of ownership for 1324 Elm Street, Any Town, Any State 45678. This document is known as:

a) affidavit

b) quitclaim deed

c) title

d) trustee deed

91. Gerard has a 30-year loan in which his interest rate is 5% for five years, then increases to 6% for the life of the loan. What type of mortgage does he have?

a) fixed rate mortgage

b) modification

c) two-step mortgage

d) fully amortized

92. The buyers purchasing Geoff's vacation home love his furnishings so much they want to buy all of them. What contract should he use for the sale of the furnishings?

a) bill of sale

b) grant deed

c) purchase and sale agreement

d) quitclaim deed

93. Real estate often deals with two main types of property. One type is personal property, what is the other type?

a. homeowner property

b. real property

c. building property

d. city-owned property

94. Which is the best description of a real estate agent?

a) anyone, licensed or not, who conducts and/or negotiates the sale of real estate

b) the owner and manager of a real estate firm

c) a person who sells both home warranties and property

d) a person who is licensed who conducts and negotiates the sale of real estate

95. Ricky's friend Esther is leaving the country. She has a great loan with a 3.5% interest rate and a remaining term of 20 years. Because Ricky would like to take over this loan, he sends her lender all of his income and asset documents. Ricky is trying to get a(n) _____.

a) primary mortgage

b) assumption

c) refinance

d) equity loan

96. A legal document which conveys title to a property is known as a:

a) deed

b) preliminary title report

c) purchase and sale agreement

d) promissory note

97. Which is the most common type of bankruptcy?

a) Chapter 13

b) Chapter 7 no assets

c) Chapter 13 no assets

d) Chapter 7

98. Someone's credit history report is prepared by a(n) _____.

a) mortgage broker

b) underwriter

c) credit bureau

d) notary public

99. Paula made her mortgage payment 30 days past her due date. Her mortgage is now in:

a) arrears

b) default

c) foreclosure

d) bankruptcy

100. What is the term for the age an appraiser uses to describe a property's physical condition?

a) effective age

b) longevity

c) year built

d) average age

Real Estate Sales Exam III Answers

1. a. There are different methods of determining value. Depreciation is shown in the book value.

2. d. In Texas, the salesperson must take 60 core review hours after the first year and 15 hours of continuing education. This renews the license for two years.

3. c. Inactive licensees must pay fees, complete applications, and take necessary continuing education courses.

4. b. RESPA limits the amount of advance property tax and insurance that can be kept in a reserve account. The amount is 1/6th of a year or two months.

5. c. A management agreement is between the owner of income property and the property manager and details the scope of work expected to be done by the property manager.

6. a. The Equal Credit Opportunity Act protects against discrimination in lending.

7. c. They are doing the mortgaging, so they are the mortgagor.

8. d. Coops are transferred as shares of stock in which there is no recording and because of this, individual property taxes are not created for each unit, but rather the coop or corporation pays a property tax bill for the entire development and passes along each member's portion to be paid through each member's monthly maintenance fee.

9. b. The cut trees are moveable so they are personal property.

10. c. A vendee is also known as the purchaser.

11. a. In order to file for adverse possession, you must prove you have continuously used the property for three years, without any warning from the owner.

12. d. Both parties are free to renegotiate.

13. c. Equity is the difference between the value and the liens.

14. b. A contingency clause is when a certain act must be accomplished within a given amount of time.

15. a. Of the six agent responsibilities, obedience, loyalty, disclosure, confidentiality, accounting and reasonable care, the agent showed loyalty to her clients by putting their interests ahead of her own.

16. c. "Taking" is when the municipality takes action against a property owner and, through the court land process, attempts to gain ownership of the property.

17. d. FHA insures the lender against borrower default.

18. a. With a voidable contract the law gives one party an option of whether or not to proceed with the agreement.

19. c. The borrower has 20 days to reinstate a loan after receiving the certified letter.

20. b. The rural homestead protects the family from creditors. A single rural homestead is maximum 100 acres, and the family homestead is 200 acres.

21. a. The rectangular survey system.

22. d. Texas is a community property state. An agreement must be made in writing to guarantee separate property.

23. b. Mechanic's liens require compliance. Failure to comply could result in a $4,000 penalty.

24. b. Realtors are members of the National Association of Realtors and many interior designers are members of the American Society of Interior Designers.

25. d. One mill is equal to one tenth of one penny or 1/1000th of a dollar, the term is often used when expressing property tax rates.

26. c. In a right of first refusal the owner has given the holder of the right an opportunity to enter into a transaction with the owner before the owner can enter into a transaction with a third party.

27. a. Subordination agreements change the priority of a mortgage or lien.

28. d. A listing agreement is a contract between a broker and seller.

29. b. Depreciation is estimated in the cost approach.

30. c. The contract must stipulate that the agent is responsible for paying his own licensing and professional fees.

31. b. Title insurance is purchased to protect the buyer. It would take effect if there were a forgery in the chain of title.

32. b. The minimum credit score set by FHA in 2015 is 580.

33. a. She may be asked to take an ethics course through the association.

34. d. Steering is the illegal practice of directing potential homebuyers away from or to particular areas.

35. c. Vacation clubs are newer timeshare programs which give members an annual allotment of points.

36. b. The subdivision plat method uses descriptions of lots and block numbers.

37. c. With a townhome purchase, the buyer purchases the individual unit and the ground below it. In addition, each unit generally has its own roof and home amenities like garages.

38. b. Titles need to be acknowledged. This occurs when they are signed before notaries.

39. b. RESPA prohibits kickbacks.

40. a. The buyer needs to provide the survey. The other items are provided by the seller.

41. c. Parking spaces assigned to occupants are "limited" to that occupant.

42. a. Real estate forms in Texas are promulgated by TREC.

43. c. The loan commitment deadline is one of the most important deadlines.

44. d. There are three ways to file discrimination complaints: HUD in writing, complaint to attorney general, civil action in state, local, district court.

45. a. According to the Fair Housing Act, a five-unit dwelling is a multifamily dwelling. A four-unit dwelling qualifies if the owner does not live in one of the units.

46. b. The income approach is used to estimate the value of income-producing properties.

47. a. When a home appreciates, it increases in value.

48. c. Assignment is when mortgage ownership is transferred from one company to another.

49. b. A note is a promise to pay.

50. d. Oftentimes bridge loan lenders will prequalify buyers for two home loans.

51. a. Clear title is free of liens and legal questions and the legality cannot be challenged.

52. c. The borrower can lose the property due to nonpayment; the property itself is the collateral.

53. c. The adjustment date on an adjustable rate loan is the date an interest rate changes.

54. b. The earnest money deposit lets the seller know the buyer is serious.

55. c. An easement is when someone other than the owner has legal access.

56. b. Developers divide up tracts of land to create individual lots

57. a. When labor or services are provided in lieu of cash, this is known as sweat equity.

58. b. Deed-in-lieu is when the homeowner voluntarily transfers the title back to the lender in exchange for release of lien and payment.

59. a. Take the down payment and divide it by the purchase price. $68,000/$319,000 = .213 or 21%.

60. c. The down payment is generally made in the form of a cashier's check and is the initial amount that the buyer contributes upfront towards the total amount due.

61. d. Government loans are guaranteed by the Veterans Administration and Rural Housing and insured by FHA.

62. b. The individual(s) who receive title to a property is/are the grantee.

63. c. Because the home was damaged and the excessive water level resulted in significant flooding, the flood insurance will cover the damages.

64. c. A liquid asset is one that can easily be converted to cash.

65. b. The lender is the financial institution that lent the money.

66. a. Power of attorney grants an individual full or limited authority on behalf of someone else.

67. c. The principal is the amount of money borrowed along with that part of the mortgage payment that reduces the unpaid balance.

68. c. An encroachment is an illegal improvement which intrudes upon another's property.

69. d. Joint tenancy has right of survivorship by which the survivor will now receive the deceased's portion of the property.

70. b. An amortization schedule is a table that shows how much principal will be applied with each mortgage payment. It also shows the yearly balance as it decreases until it reaches zero.

71. d. With a biweekly mortgage payment, the homeowner pays half of the monthly mortgage amount every two weeks; and by the end of the year they will have paid an amount equal to 13 monthly mortgage payments.

72. c. The limit on ARM loans.

73. a. Texas is a community property state. Spouses share ownership of property equally.

74. c. A due-on-sale clause allows the lender to demand full repayment if the borrower sells the property that served as security for the loan.

75. d. A fee simple subject to a condition subsequent with right of reentry is when the grantor can go to court to get back title to his property if the grantee does not comply with the grantor's condition of ownership.

76. a. The competitive market analysis helps the licensed agent/broker to identify a range of values in a given area.

77. d. The lender will lend based on the appraised value which is $365,500. 75% of $365,500 = $274,125.

78. b. Trigger terms are disclosures that must be addressed in ads. The amount of the down payment is a trigger term.

79. c. The licensee has an obligation to keep information confidential. Not disclosing what the client is willing to pay is practicing confidentiality.

80. a. There is no transfer tax in Texas.

81. b. A budget mortgage is when the lender pulls funds from the borrower's monthly payment and sets it aside in an escrow account in order to make yearly tax and insurance payments.

82. d. While they are bound by fair housing laws and cannot discriminate based on age, gender, ethnicity/race and religion, coops do have more control than condo associations since they transfer shares of stock as opposed to real property.

83. a. In this case regression describes the fact that improvements have been made to the subject property that are much greater than the neighboring homes.

84. b. The fiduciary duty of accounting states that the agent cannot commingle funds.

85. c. A Medicaid lien is a government lien and they are exempt.

86. d. Metes description gives both a bearing and a distance.

87. a. A voluntary lien is created by the action of a lienee.

88. b. Bylaws are rules and regulations that govern associations. Condominiums are associations

89. b. Disclosure is always the best course of action. If the buyer has information that would affect a purchase, it is best to disclose even if not legally demanded because the buyer may sue.

90. c. Title is a legal document evidencing a person's right of ownership in real property.

91. c. A two-step mortgage generally starts out at a set interest rate then increases after five or seven years to a higher set rate for the duration of the loan.

92. a. A bill of sale is used in transferring personal property.

93. b. Real property refers to the land and things or items that are permanently attached to it, e.g. plant life, houses, etc. Any fixed item that can cause damage to the property when it is moved is real property. Personal property refers to property that is moveable such as furniture, and will not cause any damage to the property.

94. d. A real estate agent is a licensed person who conducts and negotiates the sale of real estate.

95. b. An assumption is when a buyer assumes the seller's mortgage.

96. a. A deed is a legal document which conveys title to property.

97. b. A Chapter 7 no assets is when the filer has no assets to pay the creditors.

98. c. A credit bureau is a third party company which prepares a summary report of an individual's credit history.

99. b. Generally, payments 30 days behind on first trust deeds are said to be in default.

100. a. The effective age is a term the appraiser uses to describe a building's physical condition.

Real Estate Sales Exam IV

1. The sum of all of Mr. Slayer's personal property and real estate at the time of his death is known as his:

a) probate

b) escheat

c) estate

d) will

2. Melody's dad, a cabinet maker, built her a beautiful entertainment unit that he securely attached to the wall five years ago. Now that she's married and she and her husband want to grow their family they have decided to move. The unit will have to remain in the home because it is a(n):

a) easement

b) trade fixture

c) appurtenance

d) fixture

3. A homeowner's insurance policy:

a) is a warranty service contract that covers repair and replacement of home appliances

b) combines hazard insurance and personal liability insurance

c) is hazard insurance

d) all of the above

4. A servicer:

a) lends money to purchase a home

b) collects mortgage payments from a borrower

c) conducts title searches

d) insures the loan in case of borrower default

5. A single family home in Texas would NOT:

a) have five units

b) be owned by private individuals who use a real estate broker

c) be legal

d) be owned by an individual who is not private

6. Three homeowners live adjacent to a body of water, but their water use rights are based on when they first used or applied for use. This is known as:

a) riparian rights

b) littoral rights

c) the doctrine of prior appropriation

d) the doctrine of adverse possession

7. A tenancy that is NOT put in place by operation of law but by the parties who expressed intent is:

a) tenancy at will

b) tenancy by the entirety

c) community property

d) tenancy in common

8. All are "improvements" except:

a) sidewalk

b) street light

c) pizza oven

d) paved road

9. Which is NOT a physical characteristic of land?

a) scarcity

b) non-homogeneity

c) immobility

d) indestructibility

10. Over several years, the Parsons' land ownership has increased by means of:

a) regression

b) accretion

c) diversion

d) avulsion

11. David allows Mike to store his pickup truck in his driveway for several weeks free of charge. David gave Mike a(n) _____.

a) acknowledgement

b) tenancy right

c) license

d) easement by prescription

12. Marty receives a notice for specific performance of a real estate contract, which is asking for:

a) an earnest money deposit

b) conveyance of the property

c) a new contract

d) a deficiency judgment

13. Which is NOT an acceptable means by which a contract can be terminated?

a) sellers decide to get a divorce during transaction

b) destruction of premises

c) mutual agreement of the parties to cancel

d) impossibility of performance

14. Timothy is out of town when his broker tries to inform him that she has a buyer for his home who has made a full price bid and given her (the broker) the $3,000 earnest money deposit. What does the broker have at this point?

a) implied contract

b) executed purchase and sale agreement

c) voidable contract

d) offer

15. Patricia, who fell behind on her mortgage payments, requested assistance from her lender. Her lender helped her by substituting her old mortgage with a newer one in which

they lowered her interest rate and extended her term. What term best describes what happened?

a) refinancing

b) novation

c) accelerating

d) none of the above

16. Which of the following statements is TRUE of a listing contract?

a) It obligates the broker to convince the seller to convey the property to the first person to make an offer.

b) It maintains that the broker act as a non-agent with a seller.

c) It is an employment contract between the broker and the principal.

d) It is an agreement that lasts indefinitely.

17. Which statement represents what an exclusive –agency listing and an exclusive-right-to-sell listing have in common?

a) Both provide for only one broker to represent the seller

b) Both are net listings

c) With both, the seller allows only one salesperson to show his property

d) With both, the seller can sell the property without paying a commission

18. Margaret's broker listed and advertised her property, to find Nathan, a ready, willing and able buyer. After reviewing the offer and sleeping on it, Margaret decided to reject the offer, telling her agent she had remorse and no longer wished to sell her home. In this case Margaret:

a) will have to pay the buyers for any damages

b) must sell the property

c) owes her broker the commission

d) is within her rights to change her mind

19. Highest and best use is:

a) the effective age of a property

b) what results in its "highest value"

c) the most marketable value

d) the book value

20. All are significant factors in comparing property with the sales comparison approach EXCEPT:

a) original purchase price

b) financing terms

c) physical appearance and condition

d) sale date

21. PITI stands for:

a) payment, insurance, taxes and investment

b) principal, insurance, tariff, interest

c) payment, interest, taxes, insurance

d) principal, interest, taxes and insurance

22. Samantha has a 15-year loan at 4.5% interest for 15 years. This is a:

a) conventional fixed rate loan

b) fixed rate loan

c) variable loan

d) pay option arm loan

23. You will use which formula to calculate the gross income multiplier (GIM):

a) GIM = annual gross income/sales price

b) GIM = rate x value

c) GIM = sales price/annual gross income

d) GIM = value/rate

24. When a property is pledged for a loan without giving up possession, this is known as:

a) substitution

b) acceleration

c) hypothecation

d) alienation

25. Greg is someone who has received training, education and is experienced in estimating real property value. His job title is a(n):

a) loan processor

b) mortgage banker

c) underwriter

d) appraiser

26. Another name for Homeowner Association dues is:

a) community property fees

b) common area assessments

c) common law dues

d) apportionments

27. A(n) _____ is when a tenant is lawfully expelled from the property.

a) aversion

 b) eviction

c) conviction

d) avulsion

28. Which does NOT describe a recorder?

a) a public official who maintains public real estate records

b) county clerk

c) transcribes real estate transactions

d) collects fees for documents filed

29. Hank and Cheri use a 1003 to:

a) apply for a mortgage loan

b) write out a land contract

c) list a property for sale

d) make an offer on a home

30. Once the appraisal was completed, Jet's lender received a CRV or Certificate of Reasonable Value. What type of loan is he getting?

a) Fannie Mae

b) FHA

c) RHS

d) VA

31. _____ and _____ are government-sponsored entities.

a) FHA and VA

b) Ginnie Mae and Freddie Mac

c) Fannie Mae and Freddie Mac

d) RHS and Agricultural Loans

32. According to Regulation Z, Jasmine has _____ to rescind the transaction.

a) 5 days

b) 3 days

c) 4 days

d) 1 day

33. An employer-sponsored tax-deferred retirement plan that homebuyers can borrow against is a:

a) 401(k)

b) 203(k)

c) 403(b)

d) a and c

34. Jumbo loans refer to conforming loans greater than _____.

a) $417,000

b) $650,000

c) $471,000

d) $617,000

35. The Fair and Accurate Credit Transactions Act of 2003 (FACTA) deals with:

a) mortgage fraud

b) commingling of funds

c) prepayment penalties

d) identity theft

36. Which statement about mortgage insurance is NOT true?

a) is also known as private mortgage insurance

b) covers the lender when a homeowner defaults

c) is required when the borrower's down payment is 20% or more

d) is included in the mortgage payment

37. The Barksdale Family just learned that the city is planning to build a small commuter airport near their family farm and their home there will sit below the flight path. They were hoping to sell the farm in a year but now fear that their values may be decreased due to:

a) functional obsolescence

b) functional regression

c) economic obsolescence

d) economic regression

38. Two years ago 17-year old Jonathan inherited five two-family homes from his late father. Now two years later, Jonathan has decided to sell one of them. If he conveys his interest in the property to a purchaser by signing a deed, the contract will be:

a) valid

b) void

c) voidable

d) invalid

39. Valid exclusive listings must include:

a) an expiration date

b) a forfeiture clause

c) an automatic renewal clause

d) a provision to allow the listing broker to appoint subagents

40. Meredith wanted Haley to know that her signature was genuine as she was signing a deed transferring ownership of her property to Haley. The declaration that Meredith made before a notary was a(n):

a) sheriff's deed

b) acknowledgment

c) promissory note

d) affidavit

41. Title to real estate can be transferred by involuntary alienation by all of the following EXCEPT:

a) escheat

b) erosion

c) seisin

d) eminent domain

42. During her closing, Hillary reviewed a legal document which requires that she repay her mortgage loan during a given period of time based on a stated interest rate. This document is known as a:

a) mortgage

b) deed of trust

c) lien

d) note

43. Zachary, whose home is set to close in two weeks, gets a call from his builder saying that his new home won't be ready for another three weeks. Zachary's realtor works out a deal where he can remain in the home one week after closing. This is known as a:

a) leasehold

b) leaseback

c) lease at will

d) lease purchase

44. A trustee is:

a) a fiduciary who controls property for the benefit of another person

b) always the executor of the estate

c) a trustworthy individual

d) an attorney

45. The best type of estate to inherit is:

a) a leasehold estate

b) a life estate

c) a fee simple estate

d) a general estate

46. The time and date a document was recorded establish:

a) chain of title

b) subrogation

c) escrow

d) priority

47. Rich sells a parcel of land to Tom. Tom quickly records the deed. If Rich tries to sell the same parcel to Kevin, which of the following statements is TRUE?

a) Tom will have to bring a quitclaim deed to court, since Rich is trying to sell the same property.

b) Kevin has been given constructive notice of the prior sale because Tom quickly recorded the deed.

c) Kevin was mailed the notice of the prior sale since Tom recorded the deed.

d) none of the above

48. The acquisition of real estate through the payment of money is:

a) a sales transaction

b) a truth-in-lending transaction

c) a purchase money transaction

d) a deed-in-lieu

49. A property sales price is a:

a) debit to the buyer and a credit to the seller

b) credit to the buyer only

c) debit to the seller and credit to the buyer

d) credit to the seller only

50. Wilma collected a security deposit from each of her tenants when they signed their lease agreements. Now that she is selling her property, who should be credited with the security deposits?

a) Wilma

b) buyer

c) tenants

d) lender

51. Because Jimmy has the right to control his property, he has a right to do all of the following EXCEPT:

a) refuse to host a neighborhood block meeting at his home

b) turn away the meter reader from the local utility company

c) put a sign in his front yard that says "no soliciting"

d) host a family barbeque

52. Two properties A and B are separated by a private road. Landowner A owns the road but Landowner B has unrestricted access, as he needs to use the road to reach the main highway. What type of access does Landowner B have?

a) an easement by necessity

b) an encroachment

c) an easement

d) an assessment

53. When a deed of trust is not issued, who typically acquires the title after the money is borrowed to purchase property?

a) trustee

b) the seller's lender

c) the buyer

d) the seller

54. Contracts for the sale of real property, under the statute of frauds, must be:

a) in writing to be enforceable

b) on purchase and sale agreement forms

c) started by a licensed agent

d) executed right away

55. The Martins enter into a sales contract with the Haggardy family in which they will pay the Haggardy family $1,500 per month for their family farm. The Martins will pay all insurance premiums, property taxes, and any maintenance and repair costs, but the Haggardys will maintain title to the property for 20 years. What type of contract do the two families have?

a) lease with option to buy

b) contract for deed

c) contract at will

d) mortgage contract

56. Harry lists his home with Broker Bill. He tells Broker Bill that as long as he receives $203,000 on the sale of his home, Broker Bill can keep the difference as commission. This type of listing is known as:

a) an exclusive-agency listing

b) an open listing

c) an exclusive right-to-sell listing

d) net listing

57. The original capital outlay for labor, materials, and land is known as:

a) the market value

b) the market price

c) mortgage value

d) cost

58. Kenny, a single man, died and left all of his real estate to his niece, 23-year-old Ashley in his will. The title passes to Ashley at what point?

a) when she executes a new deed to all of the properties

b) after she pays all of the property taxes

c) immediately after Kenny's death

d) once she receives a title report that the properties are free and clear

59. How does a condominium differ from a planned unit development (PUD)?

a) a condominium usually has a pool and gym

b) in a PUD, an owner owns the building or unit he lives in

c) a PUD has more units

d) all of the above are true

60. A rate and term refinance:

a) is also known as a no cash out refinance

b) generally covers the previous balance plus the costs associated with obtaining the new mortgage

c) puts cash in the borrower's hands

d) both a and b

61. Existing mortgages are usually bought as a "pool" on the _____.

a) primary market

b) secondary market

c) government market

d) black market

62. Liens and encumbrances shown on the title commitment, other than those listed in the contract, must be removed so that the title can be conveyed free and clear. It is the _____ responsibility to remove these.

a) seller's

b) buyer's

c) lender's

d) title company's

63. The principal amount of the buyer's new mortgage is a:

a) debit to the real estate company

b) credit to the real estate company

c) credit to the buyer

d) debit to the seller

64. Jay's lender would like to ensure that he is paying a fair price for the home he is purchasing. In order to determine this, the lender will order a(n):

a) appraisal

b) broker price opinion

c) comparative market analysis

d) chain of title

65. For tax purposes, a(n) _____ establishes the value of a property.

a) broker

b) recorder

c) appraiser

d) assessor

66. Which tenancy automatically renews itself at each expiration?

a) tenancy at sufferance

b) tenancy for years

c) tenancy from month to month

d) tenancy at will

67. A valid lease has all of the requirements EXCEPT:

a) valuable consideration

b) offer and acceptance

c) capacity to contract

d) county clerk recording

68. Money set aside for the replacement of common property in a condominium or cooperative project is called:

a) replacement reserve fund

b) savings fund

c) capital improvements fund

d) contingency fund

69. Judith had to replace her boiler. This type of repair is classified as which type of maintenance?

a) construction

b) corrective

c) preventive

d) routine

70. Which does NOT affect zoning?

a) The principle of conformity enhances value.

b) The city requests that new building conform to specific types of architecture.

c) Values have remained the same because owners have the freedom to develop land as they please.

d) A new city ordinance mandates that the street floors of an office building be used for delis and cafes.

71. Happy Family Realty received a *lis pendens* for their recent listing located at 7892 Oak Street. They now have:

a) a notice of special assessment

b) a notice that legal action has been filed which could affect the property

c) a loan commitment letter

d) a home inspection report

72. New agent Barbara was so excited to close her first client that she gave her friend Nicholas $200 for referring the client to her. What Barbara did was:

a) give Nicholas what is considered a kickback and is illegal under RESPA

b) legal as it's the cost of doing business

c) as long as Barbara had her attorney draw up an agreement between her and Nicholas, this was legal

d) illegal because she should have given the money to her broker

73. Which is an example of a unilateral contract?

a) a real estate sales contract

b) an agreement which states that you will provide sweat equity as your contribution in having your home built

c) a contract between a broker and his agent

d) The sales manager says he will offer a 20% bonus if you sell $3.5 million in real estate.

74. The Gramm-Leach-Bliley Act (GLBA) requires that companies give consumers privacy notices. Which jurisdiction does this fall under?

a) The Equal Credit Opportunity Act

b) Community Reinvestment Act

c) The Federal Trade Commission

d) The Sherman Antitrust Law

75. All are loan payment plans EXCEPT:

a) 30-year fixed loan at 5.5% interest rate

b) 2-1 buy down

c) reverse mortgage

d) graduated payment mortgage

76. A primary mortgage loan is funded by:

a) a mortgage banker

b) a mortgage broker

c) both a and b

d) neither a nor b

77. What should an owner of an apartment complex do if he has determined that his vacancy rate is less than 4%?

a) Nothing

b) He should lower his advertising budget.

c) He should make property improvements.

d) He should survey the rental market to determine whether he can raise his rents.

78. Jacob and Leslie have a beautiful 2,700 square foot home just outside the city, but most of the other homes are about 1,800 square feet. Their home value has decreased because of what appraisal principle?

a) regression

b) assemblage

c) diminishing and increasing returns

d) contribution and conformity

79. Under FIRREA appraisers need to be licensed by the _____ in order to appraise real property valued over $1,000,000 in federal transactions.

a) state

b) federal government

c) county

d) bank

80. Justin dies without a will. He has no spouse or children. Who would inherit?

a) state

b) friend

c) nurse

d) niece

81. A buyer's agent should NOT disclose which of the following to the seller?

a) the relationship between the buyer and the agent

b) agent compensation that will be paid from the broker's commission

c) that the agent may benefit from referring the parties to a subsidiary of the broker's firm

d) that the buyer is anxious to find a place to live

82. The art of weighing the findings and analyzing the results from three approaches to value is known as:

a) substitution

b) reconciliation

c) assumption

d) capitalization

83. A prospective buyer is attracted to a property that has a negative cash flow. The following is likely to be TRUE?

a) the depreciable base is large

b) there is no deferred maintenance

c) there is a substantial increase in property value

d) the new buyer will have to make a huge down payment

84. What provision can stop Cary from losing her home to foreclosure if she files for Chapter 13 bankruptcy?

a) automatic stay provision

b) automatic stop provision

c) repayment provision

d) payment restructure provision

85. What type of loan is funded in the private sector?

a) secondary

b) conventional

c) FNMH

d) all of them

86. A lease does not have to be written and signed if it is shorter than _____.

a) 2 years

b) 6 months

c) 5 years

d) 1 year

87. Where should a lessor conduct an interview?

a) over the phone

b) it does not matter

c) onsite

d) interviews are not necessary

88. In some states the sellers must sign the seller's disclosure. In Texas:

a) sellers are required to sign the disclosure

b) sellers must disclose ALL defects

c) sellers are not required to sign the disclosure

d) sellers do not have to disclose a known leak

89. A licensee is found guilty of a crime. Who determines the fate of her license?

a) district court

b) TREC

c) TRELA

d) RESPA

90. What guides broker responsibility in Texas?

a) Canons of Professional Ethics and Conduct

b) Texas Occupation Code

c) RESPA

d) Texas Real Estate Commission

91. Which of the following is considered real property?

a. oak tree

b. swing set

c. couch

d. curtains

92. All are public records that may not be found through a title search EXCEPT:

a) mistakes in recording legal documents

b) unpaid liens

c) forged deed

d) fraud

93. A broker uses a PO Box for an address for TREC. What does this violate?

a) place of business

b) accountability

c) confidentiality

d) loyalty

94. Which is used as a sign of good faith?

a) home inspection

b) financing contingency

c) earnest money deposit

d) review of the purchase and sale agreement by an attorney

95. Ownership of a property by one person is known as:

a) remainder interest

b) entirety

c) severalty

d) reversionary interest

96. The words of conveyance in a deed are in the:

a) purchase clause

b) selling clause

c) granting clause

d) heading

97. Which of the following property will have the highest capitalization rate?

a) a modernized school

b) an SFR

c) a convenience store

d) a small shopping center with limited traffic access

98. Open listings are also known as:

a) multiple listings

b) nonexclusive agreements

c) exclusive rights to sell

d) net listings

99. Gilbert defaulted on his loan and the lender foreclosed. Which clause requires the lender to look only to the property for satisfaction of debt?

a) exculpatory clause

b) deficiency judgment

c) acceleration clause

d) defeasance clause

100. Grantees are protected by express covenants found in:

a) bill of sale deed

b) quitclaim deed

c) general warranty deed

d) sheriff's deed

Real Estate Sales Exam IV Answers

1. c. The sum total of an individual's personal and real property at the time of death.

2. d. A fixture is personal property that is attached to the real property.

3. b. A homeowner's insurance policy combines hazard insurance and personal liability insurance.

4. b. A servicer collects mortgage payments from a borrower.

5. a. A single-family dwelling is defined by the Fair Housing Act. Five units are included in multifamily dwellings.

6. c. The doctrine of prior appropriation is generally in areas of water scarcity. Water rights are assigned priority based on when the right was either first used or applied for.

7. b. Tenancy by the entirety is a tenancy a husband and wife can choose that is typically not recognized in community property states.

8. c. A trade fixture is an installed item that the tenant can take when they end their lease.

9. a. Scarcity is an economic characteristic of land.

10. b. Accretion is the addition of land when sand or soil is naturally deposited from rivers, streams or lakes.

11. c. Permission was granted for a specified period of time.

12. b. A suit for specific performance, oftentimes, is when there is a defaulting party. In this case the non-defaulting party is suing to force the defaulting party to carry out the terms of the contract.

13. a. Reasons to discharge a contract include: operation of law, impossibility of performance, mutual agreement of the parties to cancel, substantial performance, partial performance.

14. d. At this point the broker has a signed offer to present to the seller.

15. b. Novation occurs when the lender substitutes a new obligation for an old one.

16. c. A listing is an employment contract in which the broker provides professional services to the client.

17. a. Both the exclusive-agency and the exclusive right-to-sell listings have only one broker.

18. c. Since the broker performed, she owes the commission.

19. b. Highest and best value is the most probable use to which a property is used or suited that results in its "highest value."

20. a. Original purchase price is not compared when using the sales comparison approach.

21. d. PITI stands for principal, interest, taxes and insurance.

22. b. In a fixed rate loan the interest rate stays the same for the duration of the loan.

23. a. Gross Income Multiplier = annual gross income/sales price

24. c. When a property is pledged for a loan without giving up possession this is known as hypothecation.

25. d. An appraiser is an individual who is qualified by training, education and experience to estimate value.

26. b. Common area assessments are also known as homeowner association dues.

27. b. Eviction is when a tenant is legally expelled from the property.

28. c. A recorder is a county clerk who collects fees for documents filed as well as maintains public real property records.

29. a. A 1003 is the loan application form most often used by lenders.

30. d. In a VA loan transaction, once the appraisal is done the VA issues a Certificate of Reasonable Value.

31. c. Fannie Mae and Freddie Mac are government sponsored entities that were chartered by Congress.

32. b. Regulation Z gives most borrowers three days to rescind the transaction.

33. d. 403(b) and 401(k) are employer-sponsored investment plans.

34. a. Conventional loan amounts below $417,000 are conforming.

35. d. FACTA was designed to enhance the accuracy of borrower financial information, fight identity theft, and expand consumer access to credit.

36. c. Mortgage insurance is required when the LTV is greater than 80%.

37. c. Economic obsolescence is when a property loses value due to surrounding factors such as environmental and social forces.

38. a. The conveyance will be valid as his age at the time will be 19.

39. a. Listing agreements must have "from and to" dates.

40. b. An acknowledgment is a formal declaration before a public official such as a notary public.

41. c. Involuntary alienation transfers are generally carried out by operation of law.

42. d. A note is a legal document requiring a borrower to repay a mortgage loan during a specified period of time at a stated interest rate.

43. b. A leaseback is where a seller conveys the property to a buyer and the seller leases the property back from the buyer.

44. a. A trustee is a fiduciary who controls property for the benefit of another person.

45. c. A fee simple estate is an unconditional unlimited estate of inheritance.

46. d. Time and date of recording establish priority.

47. b. Constructive notice is based on the legal presumption that an individual may obtain information by diligent inquiry.

48. c. A purchase money transaction is the acquisition of real estate.

49. a. Property sales price results in a credit to the seller and a debit to the buyer.

50. b. The buyer should receive the security deposit credit once the deed is transferred to her.

51. b. Utility companies i.e. those companies which own the equipment, are generally granted an easement as they have a right to enter and work on the property.

52. a. An easement by necessity is an easement granted by law and court action that is necessary for full enjoyment of the land.

53. c. In Texas, the title is given to the purchaser after money is borrowed. This makes foreclosure difficult.

54. a. The law goes back to the English Common Law and demands that contracts be signed to be valid.

55. b. Contract for deed, also known as a land contract, is where the buyer pays installments to the seller for a specified period of time, but the seller maintains title to the property during that time.

56. d. A net listing is based on the net price the seller will receive if the property is sold.

57. d. Cost is the original capital outlay for labor, land, and materials.

58. c. A will takes effect upon the death of the decedent.

59. b. In a condominium the owner owns the airspace in his unit.

60. c. A cash out refinance puts funds into the hands of the borrower.

61. b. The secondary market is where "pools" of existing mortgages are bought and sold.

62. a. The seller must pay off and/or remove any liens before the title can be delivered free and clear.

63. c. The principal amount is the buyer's credit as this is what will be used to purchase the property.

64. a. The lender will order an appraisal which will be done by an appraiser, someone who has been trained and educated and is experienced in estimating value.

65. d. A public official who establishes the value for tax purposes is an assessor.

66. c. Month-to-month tenancy renews itself at each expiration.

67. d. A lease does not need to be recorded.

68. a. Money set aside for the replacement of common property in a condominium or cooperative project is called a replacement reserve fund.

69. b. Corrective maintenance involves the repair of the building's equipment.

70. c. Zoning is a tool for implementing a local plan to prevent incompatible land uses.

71. b. A *lis pendens* is a legal notice that a suit has been filed which could affect the property.

72. a. Per RESPA, kickbacks are illegal.

73. d. A unilateral contract is when a promise is exchanged for performance.

74. c. The GLBA falls under the jurisdiction of the Federal Trade Commission.

75. a. A fixed rate loan is structured for the repayment of borrowed funds.

76. a. A mortgage banker is a firm that can originate, sell, and service mortgage loans.

77. d. A vacancy rate lower than 5% generally indicates that rents are too low.

78. c. Improvements can reach a point beyond which they no longer add value but rather diminish the returns.

79. a. Under FIRREA appraisers need to be licensed by the state in order to appraise real property valued over $1,000,000 in federal transactions.

80. d. If there is no spouse or children, the estate goes to siblings and their children.

81. d. Confidentiality is an agent responsibility.

82. b. Reconciliation is the art of weighing the findings and analyzing from three approaches to value.

83. c. Negative cash flow can be offset by an increase in property value.

84. a. Chapter 13 bankruptcy has an automatic stay provision.

85. b. Conventional loans are not guaranteed. They are funded by the private sector.

86. d. Leases may be oral or written. They do not have to be signed if they are shorter than a year.

87. c. Lessors need to be careful in choosing lessees. Conducting interviews onsite will help choose the right lessees.

88. a. In Texas, sellers must sign and date disclosures.

89. b. The TREC oversees licensing. Only the TREC has the authority to revoke a license.

90. a. Canons of Professional Ethics and Conduct are used to guide the conduct of brokers in Texas.

91. a. Real property is what cannot be moved without causing damage to the property. Moving an oak tree off of the property would cause severe damage to the land.

92. b. Unpaid liens are generally found in a title search.

93. a. The place of business must be listed. It must be a physical address and not a PO Box.

94. c. The earnest money deposit is not a condition of an offer to purchase a home. It lets the seller know the buyer is serious about purchasing the home.

95. c. Severalty means that all others have been severed or cut off.

96. c. The words of conveyance can be found in the granting clause.

97. d. Because traffic is limited, the shopping center will have the greatest risk and therefore the highest cap rate.

98. b. Open listings are also known as nonexclusive agreements.

99. a. With an exculpatory clause in place the buyer is not personally liable for the debt because the clause creates a nonrecourse loan.

100. c. General warranty deeds contain covenants that warrant the new owner's clear and undisturbed title.

53104754R00120

Made in the USA
Lexington, KY
21 June 2016